PRIDE OF KENTUCKY

GREAT RECIPES WITH FOOD, FARM, AND FAMILY TRADITIONS

A partnership project of the University of Kentucky Cooperative Extension Service
and the Kentucky Department of Agriculture

PRIDE OF KENTUCKY

GREAT RECIPES WITH FOOD,
FARM, AND FAMILY TRADITIONS

Published by Kentucky Extension Association
of Family and Consumer Sciences

Copyright © 2003
by Kentucky Extension Association
of Family and Consumer Sciences
P.O. Box 446
Franklin, Kentucky
42135-0446

The Kentucky farm scene cover photograph
has been contributed by noted Kentucky
photographer James Archambeault.

Blue Ribbon Beef photo
courtesy of Harold Kelley

Selected photographs in the book are
from the 2002 Kentucky Agriculture
Photo Contest participants: Jeff Botts,
Melanie Clark, Kathy Hancock,
David Sharpe, and Kathy Jo Stubblefield.
Many heritage photographs are
from the collection of Joe Williams,
retired Extension Specialist in
Agriculture Communications.

Library of Congress Control Number:
2003103678
ISBN: 0-9728024-0-1

Edited, Designed, and Manufactured by
Favorite Recipes® Press
An imprint of

FRP

P.O. Box 305142
Nashville, Tennessee 37230
800-358-0560

Art Director: Steve Newman
Book Design: Jim Scott
Project Editor: Linda Jones

Manufactured in the
United States of America
First Printing: 2003
7,500 copies

TABLE OF CONTENTS

Symbols are used throughout
Pride of Kentucky to
designate the following:

Denotes Chef or Guest Recipe

Denotes Food Preparation

Denotes Kentucky Food Culture

Denotes Agri-Tourism

UNIVERSITY OF KENTUCKY

The *Pride of Kentucky* book is filled with great recipes that feature both traditional and newer Kentucky commodities. We are proud that our farmers continue to improve production and diversify enterprises, providing consumers with a variety of high-quality, safe, healthy, and economical foods. We are also proud that food and agriculture remain at the heart of our state's rich culture, so we have included entertaining stories about food traditions, festivals, and agri-tourism locations you can visit to experience a part of our rural heritage.

As the Dean of the University of Kentucky College of Agriculture, I want to thank each commodity group and organization for their support of this project. Thanks also to the Cooperative Extension Service Family and Consumer Sciences Agents for their work in making this book a reality. We are proud of their work and the many programs that have enriched the lives of Kentucky families since 1913.

As you browse this book and sit down to the table to sample the great recipes, you'll know why we say our food producers and farm families are the "Pride of Kentucky."

M Scott Smith

Dr. M. Scott Smith,
Dean and Director of the University of Kentucky
College of Agriculture

This cookbook promotes the best of Kentucky home cooking and much more. It also provides stories and photos about agri-tourism destinations and the culture of Kentucky farms, family, and food.

Inside these pages, you'll find recipes highlighting the best of all Kentucky commodities, from Premium Poultry, to Blue Ribbon Beef, to Prize-Winning Pork and Kentucky Fresh Produce. You'll also find recipes for Kentucky catfish, freshwater shrimp, and great dairy dishes.

As Commissioner of the Kentucky Department of Agriculture, I'm excited about how Kentuckians are responding to our Kentucky Fresh campaign, where homegrown produce is clearly marked in major supermarkets around the Commonwealth. Consumers like you want fresh produce, especially when it supports our Kentucky producers. When it comes to seafood, you have supported our marketing efforts to promote Kentucky catfish and freshwater shrimp.

Sample these recipes and sample the *Pride of Kentucky*, from farm to table and shelf to chef.

Billy Ray Smith

Commissioner Billy Ray Smith,
Kentucky Department of Agriculture

INTRODUCTION

Today's County Extension Agents for Family and Consumer Sciences continue the long tradition of the Cooperative Extension Service to teach nutrition, food preparation, safety, and preservation to families of Kentucky. Equipment and techniques have changed with the times, but the importance of good nutrition for healthy families has remained the same.

The *Pride of Kentucky* cookbook is a project of the Kentucky Extension Association of Family and Consumer Sciences (KEAFCS). KEAFCS is a professional organization of Family and Consumer Sciences employees of the University of Kentucky College of Agriculture, and Kentucky State University Cooperative Extension Service. There are Extension Agents for Family and Consumer Sciences in all 120 counties of Kentucky. We're your neighbors and friends. We live and work in your community. We serve as an extension of the state's land grant universities, the University of Kentucky and Kentucky State University, to provide information and teach skills to help people improve their lives.

The *Pride of Kentucky* project is part of our educational programming. This book is a great resource of information about purchasing and using high-quality, safe Kentucky commodities to reach nutritional recommendations for better health. It also contains stories about the rich food heritage of our state and gives information about agri-tourism sites and festivals to visit. In addition, marketing opportunities for Kentucky producers will be enhanced as consumers learn more about the diverse agriculture commodities and how to use them. The funds generated through the sale of the book will be used to expand educational programming across the state and enhance professional development of agents.

Since 1912, the University of Kentucky College of Agriculture has provided staff to teach basic skills and research-based information to the citizens across Kentucky. Early work centered on a demonstration train carrying a staff of lecturers and movable schools, with classes that usually lasted three or four days. Demonstration work during the early days focused largely on food preservation with the establishment of canning clubs to give instructions on how to can tomatoes. Health, sanitation, and clothing construction were other early areas of programming.

After the Smith-Lever Act was passed by Congress in 1914, the scope of home economics extension programming increased rapidly. Home Demonstration Agents were hired to work in individual counties and formed Home Demonstration Clubs as a network for informal education. By 1938, the number of agents had increased significantly, and the group formed the Kentucky Home Demonstration Agents Association. The Extension Agent's role as a professional educator changed over the years, as did the title. The name of the professional development organization also changed— first to the Kentucky Association of Extension Home Economists and in 1995 to the current name of Kentucky Extension Association of Family and Consumer Sciences.

We have seen many changes through the years; however, our job remains that of helping people help themselves by using the research, technology, and educational skills of the land grant university system. As County Extension Agents and Extension professionals for Family and Consumer Sciences, we work in all 120 counties across the state, and we know about our plentiful supply of high-quality, safe, nutritious agricultural products; our diverse food culture and rural traditions; and the wonderful places that showcase our agriculture industry. From Paducah to Pikeville, Covington to Corbin, and all the communities in between, we are pleased to share the best of the Commonwealth with you through the *Pride of Kentucky* cookbook.

NEAFCS

National Extension
Association of Family
and Consumer Sciences
Kentucky Affiliate

Sponsors

We offer our sincere thanks to each of the sponsors listed here. Your support has made it possible to showcase Kentucky's agricultural products through this collection of great recipes and stories about our food and farm traditions. Special acknowledgement is given to the University of Kentucky Cooperative Extension Service, the Kentucky Department of Agriculture, and the members of the Kentucky Extension Association of Family and Consumer Sciences for their financial and in-kind support, recipes and stories shared, and unfailing enthusiasm.

BEST OF SHOW

Kentucky Cattlemen's Association

Kentucky Beef Council

Kentucky Farm Bureau

Kentucky Soybean Association and Promotion Board

West Kentucky Corporation

CHAMPION LEVEL

Kentucky Pork Producers Association
Kentucky Poultry Federation/Kentucky Egg Council

PREMIUM LEVEL

Kentucky Aquaculture Association
Kentucky Association of Electric Cooperatives, Inc.
Kentucky Extension Homemakers Association

AWARD LEVEL

Kentucky Jersey Cattle Club
Kentucky Sweet Sorghum Producers and Processors Association
Lincoln Trail Area Extension Association of Family and Consumer Sciences
Weisenberger Mills, Inc.

BLUE RIBBON BEEF
Roasts · Steaks · Ground Beef

Sponsors: Kentucky Cattlemen's Association and Kentucky Beef Council

Blue Ribbon Beef

Roasts · Steaks · Ground Beef

4-H'ers proudly show their reserve and Champion Polled Hereford heifers at the 1972 Kentucky State Fair.

Kentucky is the largest beef cattle state east of the Mississippi River and ranks eighth nationally in beef cattle production. Cattle are produced in every county in the state, and cattle production represents a multi billion-dollar industry in Kentucky. Excellent climate, forage, and shipping location all combine to make the state a prime location to raise and market beef cattle. Today's cattlemen are producing more beef with 25 percent fewer cows than twenty-six years ago. Improved management of genetics and better overall herd management have resulted in a much leaner product.

Much of the success of the beef cattle industry can be attributed to the Kentucky Beef Cattle Association that is now the Kentucky Cattlemen's Association. Formed by the merger of the two parent groups, the Kentucky Cattlemen's Association and the Feeder Calf Association, the group mainly emphasized the activities that the parent organizations had begun, such as sales and bull tests. Other activities were fairly limited until Kentucky producers passed a checkoff program in 1976. The funds generated from this program were to be used for in-state promotion, and the initial focus was strictly on raising better beef cattle.

The Kentucky Cattlemen's Association is the catalyst for the state's multi-billion-dollar beef industry. This nonprofit organization serves both as the trade association, which is member driven, and as the qualified state beef council. The Kentucky Beef Council has made many inroads into retail food service by working with chefs and meat departments at local groceries. Expanded consumer programs highlight the nutritional benefits of beef and provide recipes, preparation tips, and serving suggestions. Additional programs have targeted the state's dietitians, physicians, educators, and youth groups.

These efforts to strengthen and expand both the production and consumption component of the beef industry will help secure Kentucky's place as a leader in the industry and provide significant cash receipts to producers throughout the state.

Two-Way Shredded Beef

1 medium onion, cut into quarters
3 garlic cloves
1 (3- to 3¼-pound) boneless beef
    chuck shoulder or bottom round
    roast, cut into 4 pieces

1 teaspoon salt
½ teaspoon pepper
¾ cup water

Place the onion, garlic and beef in a slow cooker. Sprinkle with the salt and
pepper. Add the water. Cook, covered, on Low for 9 to 9½ hours or until the
beef is tender. Remove the beef from the cooking liquid and cool slightly. Strain
the cooking liquid, reserving the liquid and discarding the solids. Skim the top
of the reserved liquid. Trim the beef. Shred the beef using 2 forks. Divide the
shredded beef into 2 equal portions. Add ¼ cup of the reserved cooking liquid
to each portion. Use to prepare Tex-Mex Beef Wraps or Honey Mustard Barbecue
Beefwiches. (You may store, covered, in the refrigerator for up to 4 days.)
Yield: 8 servings.

Tex-Mex Beef Wraps

½ cup frozen whole kernel corn
1 small tomato, chopped
1 tablespoon chopped cilantro
1 (16-ounce) jar thick-and-chunky
    salsa

½ recipe Two-Way Shredded Beef
    (above)
2 tablespoons chopped cilantro
4 (10-inch) flour tortillas, warmed

Combine the corn, tomato, 1 tablespoon cilantro and 2 tablespoons of the
prepared salsa in a bowl. Chill, covered, in the refrigerator until ready to serve.
     Combine the Two-Way Shredded Beef, remaining prepared salsa and 2
tablespoons cilantro in a 1½-quart microwave-safe dish. Microwave, covered,
on High for 7 to 8 minutes or until heated through, stirring once. Spoon ¼ of
the beef mixture evenly over each tortilla, leaving a 1½-inch border around the
edge. Top each with ¼ cup of the corn mixture. Fold the right and left edges of
the tortilla over the filling. Fold the bottom edge up and roll up. Garnish with
additional chopped cilantro and serve immediately. *Yield: 4 servings.*

COOK BEEF SAFELY

Cooking food to the proper temperature kills harmful bacteria and prevents food borne illness. Use a food thermometer to check the internal temperature. These are the recommended temperatures for thorough cooking:

- *Hamburger and ground beef—160 degrees*
- *Roasts and steaks medium-rare— 145 degrees*
- *Roasts and steaks medium—160 degrees*
- *Roasts and steaks well done—170 degrees*

HONEY MUSTARD BARBECUE BEEFWICHES

$^1/_2$ recipe Two-Way Shredded Beef
   (page 11)
1 cup honey mustard barbecue sauce
4 hamburger buns or kaiser rolls,
   split

Chopped green bell pepper
   (optional)
Chopped sweet onion (optional)

Combine the Two-Way Shredded Beef and barbecue sauce in a $1^1/_2$-quart microwave-safe dish. Microwave, covered, on High for 5 to 6 minutes or until heated through, stirring once. Spread equal amounts of the beef mixture on the bottom halves of the buns. Sprinkle with chopped green bell pepper and chopped sweet onion. Top with the remaining halves of the buns.
Yield: 4 servings.

COMPANY POT ROAST

1 (4-pound) beef rump roast
$^1/_4$ cup vegetable oil
1 cup soy sauce
2 cups water
2 cinnamon sticks
$^1/_8$ teaspoon anise seeds

1 envelope onion soup mix
$^1/_2$ cup sugar
1 cup dry sherry (optional)
3 tablespoons cornstarch
$^1/_2$ cup cold water

Brown the beef in the hot oil in a Dutch oven or large heavy skillet. Combine the soy sauce, 2 cups water, cinnamon sticks, anise seeds, onion soup mix and sugar in a bowl and mix well. Pour over the beef. Simmer, covered, for 3 hours, spooning the liquid over the beef once every hour. Add the sherry. Cook for 1 hour. Remove the beef to a warm platter. Drain the cooking liquid, reserving $2^1/_2$ cups. Strain the liquid if desired, discarding the solids.

Mix the cornstarch and $^1/_2$ cup cold water in a small bowl. Bring the reserved liquid to a boil and reduce the heat. Stir in the cornstarch mixture. Simmer until thickened, stirring constantly. Spoon over the beef. Serve with rice or poppy seed noodles. *Yield: 12 servings.*

FIESTA BEEF POT ROAST

1 cup uncooked long grain white rice
1 teaspoon chili powder
1/2 cup frozen corn
1/4 cup thick-and-chunky salsa
2 tablespoons chopped fresh cilantro

1 (2- to 2 1/2-pound) package
    fully cooked boneless beef
    pot roast with gravy
3/4 cup thick-and-chunky salsa

Cook the rice using the package directions, adding the chili powder. Remove from the heat. Stir in the corn, 1/4 cup salsa and cilantro. Cover and let stand for 5 minutes.

Prepare the beef using the package directions. Remove the beef to a serving platter and keep warm. Pour the gravy into a saucepan. Add 3/4 cup salsa and mix well. Cook until heated through. Serve the beef with the rice and gravy.
Yield: 6 servings.

BELLEFONT BEEF CURRY

1 onion, sliced
1 1/2 tablespoons vegetable oil
2 to 3 teaspoons curry powder
1 1/2 pounds lean beef cubes
8 ounces mushrooms, sliced
1 tomato, chopped, or 1 (15-ounce)
    can diced tomatoes

1 garlic clove, minced
2 teaspoons salt
2 teaspoons sugar
2 cups water
2 tablespoons cornstarch
2 tablespoons water

Sauté the onion in the hot oil in a skillet until tender. Stir in the curry powder. Cook for 1 minute. Add the beef, mushrooms, tomato, garlic, salt and sugar. Cook until the beef is light brown. Add 2 cups water. Cook for 2 hours over low heat. Mix the cornstarch and 2 tablespoons water in a bowl. Stir into the beef mixture. Cook until thickened, stirring constantly. Serve with hot cooked rice.
Yield: 4 servings.

EASY BEEF TIPS

1 tablespoon dark sesame oil
1 (16-ounce) package frozen broccoli stir-fry vegetables (broccoli, carrots,
　　onion, red bell peppers, celery, water chestnuts, mushrooms)
1 tablespoon minced fresh gingerroot
1 garlic clove, minced
$1/8$ teaspoon crushed red pepper
1 (17-ounce) package fully cooked beef tips with gravy
$1/3$ cup water
2 cups hot cooked rice

Heat the sesame oil in a large nonstick skillet over medium heat until hot. Add
the vegetables, ginger, garlic and red pepper. Stir-fry for 2 to 3 minutes. Stir in
the beef tips with gravy and the water. Bring to a boil. Spoon over the rice.
Yield: 4 servings.

FRENCH DIP

2 cups water
$1/3$ cup bottled lemon juice
$1/3$ cup soy sauce
1 tablespoon dried onion flakes
2 teaspoons instant beef bouillon
$1/4$ teaspoon garlic powder
1 (2-pound) eye-of-round or beef brisket
6 miniature loaves French bread

Combine the water, lemon juice, soy sauce, dried onion flakes, beef bouillon,
garlic powder and beef in a slow cooker. Cook on Low for 6 to 8 hours. Cut the
beef into thin slices and place over the French bread. Serve with the remaining
liquid for dipping. Serve with wild rice and a green salad. *Yield: 6 servings.*

Roast Beef Cheddar Pockets

1 (16- to 17-ounce) package refrigerated fully cooked boneless beef pot roast
    with gravy
1 (8-count) can crescent rolls
3/4 cup (3 ounces) shredded sharp Cheddar cheese
1/3 cup finely chopped sweet onion (optional)
1/4 cup (1 ounce) shredded sharp Cheddar cheese
1/4 cup sour cream

Drain the beef, reserving the gravy for another use. Cut the beef into fine shreds. Unroll the crescent roll dough onto an ungreased baking sheet. Separate the dough into 4 rectangles, pressing the seams to seal. Pull the sides of the rectangles slightly to enlarge.

Combine the beef, 3/4 cup cheese and onion in a large bowl. Divide the beef mixture into 4 portions. Press each portion to compact and place lengthwise in the center of the rectangles. Fold the long sides of each rectangle over the filling, pressing the seams to seal. Press the ends to seal. Sprinkle evenly with 1/4 cup cheese.

Bake at 375 degrees for 13 to 16 minutes or until golden brown. Top with the sour cream. Garnish with chopped fresh chives. *Yield: 4 servings.*

Slow Cooker Stew

5 potatoes
1 (16-ounce) package baby carrots
1 pound lean beef cubes for stew
1 medium white onion, cut into quarters
1 (10-ounce) can golden mushroom soup
1 cup water

Peel the potatoes and cut into large chunks. Layer the potatoes, carrots, beef and onion in a slow cooker. Pour a mixture of the soup and water over the layers. Cook, covered, on Low for 6 to 8 hours. *Yield: 8 servings.*

GREAT GRILLED STEAKS

For great grilled steaks, grill uncovered over medium coals. Follow these guidelines for medium-rare to rare, turning occasionally.
Beef Steak, Thickness, Total Cooking Time

- *Tenderloin, 1 inch, 13 to 15 minutes*
- *Ribeye, 3/4 inch, 6 to 8 minutes*
  1 inch, 11 to 14 minutes
- *Rib, small end, 3/4 inch, 6 to 8 minutes*
  1 inch, 9 to 12 minutes
- *T-Bone or Porterhouse, 3/4 inch, 10 to 12 minutes*
  1 inch, 14 to 16 minutes
- *Top loin strip, boneless, 3/4 inch, 10 to 12 minutes*
  1 inch, 15 to 18 minutes
- *Top Sirloin, boneless, 3/4 inch, 13 to 16 minutes*
  1 inch, 17 to 21 minutes

BLUE RIBBON TENDERLOIN STEAKS WITH RED PEPPER JELLY

$^1/_2$ teaspoon chili powder
$^1/_2$ teaspoon pepper
$^1/_8$ teaspoon garlic salt
$^1/_4$ teaspoon oregano
$^1/_4$ teaspoon cumin

1 teaspoon olive oil
4 (4-ounce) beef tenderloin steaks
$^1/_2$ cup no-salt-added beef broth
$^1/_4$ cup red wine vinegar
2 tablespoons red jalapeño chile jelly

Mix the chili powder, pepper, garlic salt, oregano and cumin in a bowl. Heat the olive oil in a large nonstick skillet over medium-high heat until hot. Rub the seasoning mixture over both sides of the steaks. Add the steaks to the prepared skillet. Cook for 4 minutes on each side or to the desired degree of doneness. Remove the steaks from the skillet and keep warm. Add the broth, vinegar and jelly to the pan drippings in the skillet. Cook for 5 minutes or until slightly thickened, stirring frequently. Spoon over the steaks. *Yield: 4 servings.*

BOURBON STEAK

Kentucky Fresh

Recipe courtesy of Angie Vives, Chef,
Kentucky Lt. Governor's Mansion, Frankfort

3 tablespoons olive oil
2 tablespoons Dijon mustard
$^1/_4$ cup bourbon
$^1/_3$ cup soy sauce
2 tablespoons red wine vinegar
1 tablespoon Worcestershire sauce

$^1/_4$ cup packed brown sugar
2 tablespoons minced garlic
1 teaspoon salt
2 teaspoons pepper
1 (1$^1/_2$-pound) top round steak, 1$^1/_2$ inches thick

Combine the first 10 ingredients in a bowl and mix well. Place the steak in a sealable plastic bag. Pour the marinade over the steak and seal the bag. Marinate in the refrigerator for 6 to 12 hours. Drain the steak, discarding the marinade. Place the steak on a grill rack. Grill, uncovered, over medium-hot coals for 25 to 30 minutes for medium-rare to medium. Remove the steak to a cutting board. Let stand for 3 to 5 minutes. Cut diagonally across the grain into thin strips. Serve with roasted potatoes. *Yield: 4 servings.*

Marinated Grilled Flank Steak

Juice of 1 lemon
$^{1}/_{2}$ cup lite soy sauce
$^{1}/_{4}$ to $^{1}/_{3}$ cup dry red wine
3 tablespoons vegetable oil
2 tablespoons Worcestershire sauce

2 garlic cloves, sliced
Pepper to taste
Chopped green onions to taste
$^{1}/_{8}$ teaspoon celery seeds
1 (1$^{1}/_{2}$-pound) flank steak, trimmed

Mix the lemon juice, soy sauce, wine, oil, Worcestershire sauce, garlic, pepper, green onions and celery seeds in a bowl. Place the steak in a sealable plastic bag. Pour the marinade over the steak and seal the bag. Marinate in the refrigerator for 2 to 12 hours, turning occasionally. Drain the steak, discarding the marinade. Place the steak on a grill rack. Grill over hot coals for 5 minutes per side for rare. Cut diagonally across the grain into slices. *Yield: 6 servings.*

Stuffed Rolled Steak

1 (2-pound) round steak
1 teaspoon salt
$^{1}/_{4}$ teaspoon pepper
2 cups seasoned bread crumbs
3 tablespoons grated onion

1 teaspoon poultry seasoning
$^{1}/_{3}$ cup milk
2 tablespoons butter, melted
1 egg, beaten

Season the steak with salt and pepper. Mix the bread crumbs, onion, poultry seasoning, milk, butter and egg in a bowl. Spread evenly over the steak. Roll up to enclose the filling and tie with string. Place seam side down in a roasting pan. Bake at 350 degrees for 45 minutes or until tender. *Yield: 6 servings.*

Round Steak Sauerbraten

1 (1½- pound) round steak,
    ½ inch thick
1 tablespoon vegetable oil
1 envelope brown gravy mix
2 cups water
1 tablespoon minced onion

1 tablespoon brown sugar
2 tablespoons wine vinegar
1 teaspoon Worcestershire sauce
¼ teaspoon ginger
½ teaspoon salt
¼ teaspoon pepper

Cut the steak into 1-inch squares. Brown the steak in the hot oil in a skillet. Remove the steak from the skillet and keep warm. Add the gravy mix and water to the pan drippings in the skillet. Bring to a boil, stirring constantly. Stir in the onion, brown sugar, wine vinegar, Worcestershire sauce, ginger, salt and pepper. Return the steak to the skillet. Spoon into a 1½-quart baking dish. Bake, covered, at 350 degrees for 1½ hours. Serve over spaetzle or hot buttered noodles. *Yield: 8 servings.*

Pleasant Home Swiss Steak

1 (2-pound) boneless beef round
    steak, ¾ to 1 inch thick
3 tablespoons vegetable oil
2 cups chopped green bell pepper
1 cup chopped celery

1 cup chopped onion
1 garlic clove, minced
2 (15-ounce) cans diced tomatoes
2 tablespoons Worcestershire sauce
½ teaspoon garlic salt

Cut the beef into serving-size pieces. Heat the oil in a Dutch oven over medium-high heat. Add the beef. Cook until the beef is brown. Add the bell pepper, celery, onion and garlic. Cook for 10 minutes, stirring constantly. Add the undrained tomatoes, Worcestershire sauce and garlic salt. Cook, covered, over low to medium heat for 2 hours or until tender. *Yield: 8 servings.*

Less tender cuts of beef are best when prepared by moist heat methods such as braising and cooking in liquid. Slowly cooking arm steaks, blade pot roasts, short ribs, stew meat, brisket, and round steak in moist heat will soften the connective tissue and produce a more tender product.

SMOTHERED SWISS STEAK

1 (2-pound) round steak
1/4 cup flour
1/4 cup vegetable oil
1 cup ketchup
1 small onion, chopped
3 tablespoons sugar
1 tablespoon prepared mustard
3/4 teaspoon oregano
1/2 teaspoon chili powder
1 cup water

Cut the steak into serving pieces. Dredge in the flour. Brown evenly in the oil in a skillet. Mix the ketchup, onion, sugar, mustard, oregano and chili powder in a bowl. Spread over the steak. Add the water. Simmer, covered, over low heat until the steak is tender, adding additional water if needed. *Yield: 8 servings.*

MADRAS BEEF CURRY

2 onions, finely chopped
2 garlic cloves, minced
1 tablespoon vegetable oil
1 tablespoon curry powder
1 (1-pound) sirloin steak, cubed
1 (15-ounce) can chopped tomatoes
2 teaspoons salt
Juice of 1 lemon

Sauté the onions and garlic in the oil in a skillet for 4 minutes. Add the curry powder and beef and mix well. Cook, covered, for 10 minutes. Add the tomatoes. Simmer, covered, until the beef is tender. Stir in the salt and lemon juice. Serve over hot cooked rice. *Yield: 6 servings.*

Sonaran Beef Steak

1 cup plain dry bread crumbs
2 teaspoons taco seasoning mix
Salt and pepper to taste
4 beef cubed steaks
   (about 1 pound)

2 to 4 tablespoons garlic-flavored
   olive oil or olive oil
3/4 cup prepared ranch salad dressing
2 tablespoons chopped fresh cilantro
1 to 2 teaspoons taco seasoning mix

Mix the bread crumbs, 2 teaspoons taco seasoning mix, salt and pepper together on waxed paper. Brush the steaks with some of the olive oil. Dredge in the bread crumb mixture and press the mixture into the steaks. Heat the remaining olive oil in a 12-inch nonstick skillet over medium to medium-high heat. Add the steaks. Cook for 6 to 8 minutes or until cooked through, turning occasionally. Heat the ranch salad dressing, 2 tablespoons cilantro and 1 to 2 teaspoons taco seasoning mix in a small saucepan until heated through. Spoon over the steaks. Garnish with chopped fresh cilantro. *Yield: 4 servings.*

Ground Beef and Asparagus Pasta Toss

3 cups uncooked bow tie pasta
Salt to taste
1 pound fresh asparagus, cut into
   1-inch pieces
1 pound lean ground beef

3 tablespoons olive oil
1/4 cup minced shallots
2 garlic cloves, minced
Salt and pepper to taste
1/4 cup shredded Parmesan cheese

Cook the pasta in boiling salted water in a saucepan for 10 minutes or until almost tender. Add the asparagus. Cook for 3 to 4 minutes longer or until the pasta and asparagus are tender; drain well. Brown the ground beef in a large nonstick skillet over medium heat for 8 to 10 minutes, stirring until crumbly. Remove from the skillet with a slotted spoon. Discard the drippings in the skillet. Heat the olive oil in the skillet over medium heat. Add the shallots and garlic. Cook for 3 to 4 minutes or until tender, stirring frequently. Remove from the heat. Add the ground beef and toss to mix well. Season with salt and pepper. Combine the ground beef mixture and pasta mixture in a large bowl and toss to mix well. Sprinkle with the Parmesan cheese. *Yield: 4 servings.*

KENTUCKY COTTAGE BEEF BAKE

1 pound lean ground beef
1 (8-ounce) can tomato sauce
1 teaspoon salt
1 teaspoon pepper
¼ teaspoon garlic salt
8 ounces medium egg noodles

½ cup chopped green onions
1 cup sour cream
1 cup lite cottage cheese
¾ cup (3 ounces) shredded sharp
    Cheddar cheese

Brown the ground beef in a skillet, stirring untl crumbly; drain. Add the tomato sauce, salt, pepper and garlic salt. Simmer for 5 minutes.

Cook the noodles using the package directions. Rinse the noodles and drain well. Combine the noodles, green onions, sour cream and cottage cheese in a bowl and toss to coat.

Layer the noodle mixture and ground beef mixture ½ at a time in a 2-quart baking dish. Top with the Cheddar cheese. Bake at 350 degrees for 25 to 30 minutes or until hot and bubbly and the Cheddar cheese is melted and brown. *Yield: 8 servings.*

In the 1950s farmers focused on improved feeding and management of beef cattle operations.

SAFE GROUND BEEF

Check freshness dates when purchasing any variety of ground beef. Keep ground beef and its juices separate from other foods in your grocery cart and in your refrigerator. Refrigerate ground beef promptly after purchasing. Prepackaged fresh ground beef can be stored in the refrigerator for one to two days.

Thaw ground beef in the refrigerator or microwave— never at room temperature. Wash your hands before and after handling ground beef. Do not place cooked ground beef patties on a plate which held uncooked patties.

Always use a clean food thermometer to make sure ground beef patties are cooked to at least 160 degrees. Heat leftovers thoroughly to 165 degrees. Refrigerate leftover ground beef patties and dishes promptly.

BEEF SPAGHETTI CASSEROLE

16 ounces Cheddar cheese
6 to 8 green onions, chopped, or 1
    large onion, chopped
2 pounds lean ground beef
3 to 4 cups cooked or canned
    tomatoes
1 (4-ounce) jar mushrooms

2 tablespoons chili powder
1 teaspoon pepper
Salt to taste
8 ounces thin spaghetti, cooked and
    drained
Paprika to taste

Shred some of the cheese and reserve for the topping. Cut the remaining cheese into cubes. Sauté the green onions in a nonstick skillet until tender. Remove the green onions to a bowl. Brown the ground beef in the skillet, stirring until crumbly; drain. Drain the tomatoes, reserving the juice. Combine the green onions, ground beef, cubed cheese, tomatoes and mushrooms in a large bowl. Mix the reserved tomato juice, chili powder, pepper and salt in a small bowl. Add to the ground beef mixture and mix well. Add the spaghetti and toss to mix well. Spoon into two 2-quart baking dishes. Sprinkle with the reserved shredded cheese. Sprinkle with paprika. Bake at 350 degrees for 30 to 45 minutes or until bubbly. *Yield: 16 servings.*

SILVER GROVE SENSATIONAL STROGANOFF

1 pound lean ground beef
1/2 cup minced onion
1 garlic clove, minced
2 tablespoons flour
1 teaspoon salt
1/4 teaspoon pepper

1 (8-ounce) can sliced mushrooms,
    drained
1 (10-ounce) can cream of
    mushroom soup
1 cup sour cream

Brown the ground beef, onion and garlic in a skillet over medium heat. Stir in the flour, salt, pepper, mushrooms and soup. Cook, covered, for 5 minutes. Simmer, uncovered, for 10 minutes. Stir in the sour cream. Cook until heated through. Serve over hot cooked rice or noodles with green peas as a side dish. *Yield: 4 servings.*

MICROWAVE LASAGNA

8 ounces ground beef
1 (32-ounce) jar pasta sauce
1 teaspoon oregano
1/2 teaspoon garlic powder
15 ounces cottage cheese
1 egg, lightly beaten

1/2 teaspoon salt, or to taste
1/2 teaspoon pepper
9 uncooked lasagna noodles
8 ounces mozzarella cheese,
    shredded
1/2 cup grated Parmesan cheese

Crumble the ground beef into a microwave-safe dish. Microwave on High for 2 to 3 minutes or until brown; drain. Stir in the pasta sauce, oregano and garlic powder. Cook on High for 4 to 5 minutes. Combine the cottage cheese, egg, salt and pepper in a bowl. Spoon 1/2 cup of the ground beef mixture into a 12×18-inch microwave-safe dish. Alternate the noodles, cottage cheese mixture, mozzarella cheese and remaining ground beef mixture in the dish until all the ingredients are used. Microwave on High for 8 minutes. Microwave at Medium-Low for 20 to 22 minutes or until hot and bubbly. Sprinkle with the Parmesan cheese. Let stand for 15 minutes before serving. *Yield: 10 servings.*

METCALFE MEATBALLS

3 pounds ground round
1 (12-ounce) can evaporated milk
1 cup chopped onion
1/2 teaspoon garlic powder
2 teaspoons salt
1/2 teaspoon pepper
2 eggs, lightly beaten

2 tablespoons chili powder
2 cups rolled oats
4 cups ketchup
2 cups packed brown sugar
1 cup chopped onion
1 teaspoon garlic powder

Combine the ground round, evaporated milk, onion, garlic powder, salt, pepper, eggs, chili powder and oats in a large bowl and mix well. Shape into golf ball-size balls. Place in a 9×13-inch baking dish sprayed with nonstick cooking spray. Mix the ketchup, brown sugar, onion and garlic powder in a bowl. Pour over the meatballs. Cover with foil. Bake at 350 degrees for 1 hour or until the meatballs are cooked through. *Yield: 20 servings.*

MEAT LOAF WITH SAUCE

1½ pounds ground beef
2 slices bread, cubed
1 (15-ounce) can tomato sauce
½ cup evaporated milk
1 egg
1½ teaspoons sugar
1 teaspoon salt
1 teaspoon pepper
1 small onion, chopped
½ green bell pepper, chopped
2 tablespoons water
½ cup water
2 tablespoons Worcestershire sauce
2 tablespoons vinegar
2 tablespoons prepared mustard
2 tablespoons brown sugar

Combine the ground beef, bread, ½ of the tomato sauce, evaporated milk, egg, sugar, salt and pepper in a large bowl and mix well. Combine the onion, bell pepper and 2 tablespoons water in a medium microwave-safe bowl. Microwave, covered, for 2 minutes. Add to the ground beef mixture and mix well. Shape into a rectangular loaf in a 9×13-inch baking dish. Mix the remaining tomato sauce, ½ cup water, Worcestershire sauce, vinegar, prepared mustard and brown sugar in a bowl and mix well. Pour over the meat loaf. Bake at 350 degrees for 1 hour. Cool slightly. Cut into slices 1 inch wide and serve with the sauce. (To remove the fat, lift the meat loaf to a platter. Chill the sauce in the baking dish until the fat hardens on top. Discard the fat. Also, the meat loaf and sauce may be reheated in the microwave as needed.) *Yield: 8 servings.*

FAMILY FAVORITE MEAT LOAF

2/3 cup dry bread crumbs or
    rolled oats
1 cup milk
1 1/2 pounds ground beef
2 eggs
1/4 cup grated onion
1 teaspoon salt

1/2 teaspoon sage
1/8 teaspoon pepper
1/4 cup ketchup
3 tablespoons brown sugar
1/4 teaspoon nutmeg
1 teaspoon mustard

Soak the bread crumbs in the milk in a large bowl. Add the ground beef, eggs, onion, salt, sage and pepper and mix well. Pack into a 5×8-inch loaf pan. Mix the ketchup, brown sugar, nutmeg and mustard in a small bowl. Spread over the meat loaf. Bake at 350 degrees for 1 hour or until cooked through. (You may pack into greased muffin cups for individual meat loaves and bake for 45 minutes. Also, if you are allergic to milk, eggs or wheat, omit and use soy milk or water for the liquid and rolled oats for the bread crumbs.) *Yield: 12 servings.*

EDEN SHALE SLOPPY JOES

1 tablespoon vegetable oil or
    shortening
1/2 cup minced onion
1/2 cup chopped celery
1/2 cup chopped green bell pepper
1/2 cup shredded carrots
1 1/4 pounds ground round

1/2 cup ketchup
1/2 cup water
1 teaspoon chili powder
1/2 teaspoon salt
1/4 teaspoon pepper
1/8 teaspoon hot pepper sauce
8 whole wheat sandwich buns, split

Heat the oil in a large skillet over medium heat. Add the onion, celery, bell pepper and carrots. Sauté until tender. Add the ground round. Cook until brown and crumbly, stirring constantly; drain. Stir in the ketchup, water, chili powder, salt, pepper and hot pepper sauce. Simmer, uncovered, over low heat for 15 minutes or until thickened. Spoon onto the bottom halves of the buns. Top with the remaining halves of the buns. (This is a quick and easy meal that lets you camouflage vegetables for picky eaters.) *Yield: 8 servings.*

CLAYSVILLE CABBAGE ROLLS

3 pounds ground beef
1 pound sausage or ground pork
1¹/₂ cups rice, cooked
2 medium onions, chopped
1 teaspoon salt
¹/₂ teaspoon pepper
1 teaspoon garlic salt, or to taste
¹/₂ to 1 teaspoon hot sauce
30 large cabbage leaves
2 (15-ounce) cans sauerkraut
1 cup (or more) tomato juice
2 to 3 pounds smoked sausage, cut into 1-inch pieces

Combine the ground beef, sausage, rice, onions, salt, pepper, garlic salt and hot sauce in a bowl and mix well. Cook the cabbage leaves in a small amount of water in a large saucepan until wilted. Spoon the ground beef mixture into the cabbage leaves and roll up. Place in a 9×13-inch baking dish. Pour the undrained sauerkraut and tomato juice over the cabbage rolls. Place the smoked sausage on the top. Bake, covered, at 300 degrees for 3 to 4 hours or until cooked through. *Yield: 30 servings.*

Kentucky families of German descent often practice the tradition of serving cabbage on New Year's Day to bring blessings through the year.

PRIZE-WINNING PORK
Roasts · Chops · Sausage · Country Ham

Sponsor: Kentucky Pork Producers Association

PRIZE-WINNING PORK
Roasts • Chops • Sausage • Country Ham

HOGS ARE LEANER

1940s HOG

1990s HOG

The swine industry in Kentucky offers a great opportunity for agricultural economic growth. Hogs account for 4 percent of the total livestock receipts in Kentucky, totaling $94,321,000 gross income for Kentucky's farmers in 2001.

The Kentucky Pork Producers have been leaders in supporting a promotional arm. They have increased efforts to improve the consumers' awareness of pork as lean and nutritious, containing 31 percent less fat than pork from 1983. The checkoff funded "Pork—The Other White Meat" campaign and promotion of the diversity of pork for grilling, stir-fry, sandwich, salad, and other recipes has resulted in an increase in pork consumption. The producer organization also leads in new product development with its own Kentucky Pork Producers' "Pork Burger." They have worked to create interest and markets for Kentucky pork products around the world and especially the Pacific Rim countries. Pork products such as country ham can be promoted and sold to many foreign countries.

Like all segments of the agriculture economy, there is a trend toward larger swine units that have distinct advantages in marketing and resource procurement. However, with increased animal units in these operations, producers face new management challenges. Producers are working hand in hand with university researchers, government regulators, and environmentalists to develop systems that provide protection of the environment and maintain economic feasibility.

Cinnamon Apple Pork Roast

1 (2-pound) boneless pork loin roast
1 tablespoon vegetable oil
1 teaspoon pepper
1/2 teaspoon ginger
1/4 teaspoon nutmeg
1/4 teaspoon cinnamon
1/2 cup apple juice

1/4 cup honey
1 tablespoon lemon juice
1/2 teaspoon ginger
1/4 teaspoon nutmeg
1/4 teaspoon cinnamon
2 apples, peeled and cut into wedges

Brush the pork with the oil. Mix the pepper, 1/2 teaspoon ginger, 1/4 teaspoon nutmeg and 1/4 teaspoon cinnamon together. Rub over the surface of the pork. Place in a shallow roasting pan. Bake at 350 degrees for 45 to 60 minutes or until a meat thermometer inserted into the thickest portion registers 155 degrees. Remove from the oven. Let stand for 10 minutes or until a meat thermometer inserted into the thickest portion registers 160 degrees.

Combine the apple juice, honey, lemon juice, 1/2 teaspoon ginger, 1/4 teaspoon nutmeg and 1/4 teaspoon cinnamon in a small saucepan. Add the apple wedges. Cook over medium heat until the apples are tender.

To serve, cut the pork into slices and serve with the apple mixture.
Yield: 6 servings.

Pork Loin Roast with Bourbon Glaze

1 (2- to 2 1/2-pound) boneless
   pork loin
Salt and pepper to taste

1 (10-ounce) jar Kentucky Bourbon
   Peach Butter

Place the pork in an 8×8-inch baking dish. Rub with salt and pepper. Spoon or brush the Bourbon Peach Butter over the pork. Bake, uncovered, at 325 degrees for 1 hour or until a meat thermometer inserted into the thickest portion registers 160 degrees. Let stand before slicing. *Yield: 4 servings.*

Don't Overcook Pork

Easy does it? The most important cooking tip for pork is don't overdo it. Years ago, people believed you had to serve pork well done in order for it to be safe to eat. So the pork of the past often tasted dry and looked leathery. Today, production methods have improved. Now, most cuts should be served at medium doneness (160 degrees on a meat thermometer) for a juicy, more flavorful taste. Trichinosis is virtually nonexistent in this country due to controlled production conditions. According to the United States Department of Agriculture, the organism, if present, is destroyed well below the recommended 160-degree end temperature.

Kentucky Garlic and Rosemary Pork Tenderloin

1 (1½-pound) pork tenderloin
2 garlic cloves, sliced
1 tablespoon rosemary
2 tablespoons vegetable oil
2 tablespoons Dijon mustard
  (optional)

1 tablespoon flour or cornstarch
1 cup cold water or broth
1 tablespoon butter
1 sprig of fresh rosemary
Salt and pepper to taste

Rinse the pork under cold water and pat dry with paper towels. Pierce the pork with a knife and insert 1 slice of garlic every 1 to 2 inches. Mix 1 tablespoon rosemary and the oil in a small bowl. Rub over the surface of the pork. Rub the mustard over the pork. Place on a rack in a roasting pan. Bake, uncovered, at 350 degrees for 45 to 60 minutes or until a meat thermometer inserted into the thickest portion registers 160 degrees. Remove the pork to a serving platter, reserving 2 tablespoons of the pan drippings.

Mix the flour and cold water in a saucepan until smooth. Add the reserved drippings and mix well. Add the sprig of rosemary. Bring to a boil and reduce the heat. Cook until thickened, stirring constantly. Season with salt and pepper. Discard the sprig of rosemary before serving.

To serve, cut the pork into slices and serve with the gravy. *Yield: 4 servings.*

Holiday Pork Tenderloin

1 (16-ounce) can jellied cranberry
  sauce
⅓ cup French salad dressing

1 sweet onion, sliced
1 (3-pound) pork tenderloin

Combine the cranberry sauce, salad dressing and onion in a medium bowl and mix well. Place the pork in a slow cooker. Pour the cranberry sauce mixture over the pork. Cook on High for 4 hours or on Low for 8 hours or until a meat thermometer inserted into the thickest portion registers 160 degrees. *Yield: 6 servings.*

Grilled Pork Tenderloin

½ cup peanut oil
⅓ cup soy sauce
¼ cup red wine vinegar
3 tablespoons lemon juice
2 tablespoons Worcestershire sauce

1 garlic clove, crushed
1 tablespoon chopped fresh parsley
1 tablespoon dry mustard
1½ teaspoons pepper
2 (¾- to 1-pound) pork tenderloins

Combine the peanut oil, soy sauce, wine vinegar, lemon juice, Worcestershire sauce, garlic, parsley, dry mustard and pepper in a heavy-duty sealable plastic bag and shake to mix well. Add the pork and turn to coat. Seal the bag. Marinate in the refrigerator for 4 hours or longer, turning occasionally. Drain the pork, discarding the marinade. Place the pork on a grill rack. Grill, covered, over medium coals (300 to 400 degrees) until a meat thermometer inserted into the thickest portion registers 160 degrees. *Yield: 6 servings.*

Barbecued Pork on Buns

2 cups chopped cooked pork
¼ cup chopped green bell pepper
2 tablespoons pork drippings
½ cup ketchup
2 teaspoons prepared mustard
2 tablespoons water

2 tablespoons brown sugar
1 tablespoon instant minced onion
1 tablespoon Worcestershire sauce
½ teaspoon salt
4 hamburger buns, split

Lightly brown the pork and bell pepper in the pork drippings in a skillet; drain. Add the ketchup, mustard, water, brown sugar, onion, Worcestershire sauce and salt and mix well. Cook over low heat for 20 to 25 minutes, stirring occasionally. Spoon onto the bottom halves of the buns. Top with the remaining halves. *Yield: 4 servings.*

The phrase "pork barrel politics" is derived from the pre–Civil War practice of distributing salt pork to the slaves from huge barrels. By the 1870s, congressmen were referring to regularly dipping into the "pork barrel" to obtain funds for popular projects in their home districts.

Kentucky

DOUBLE STINK
HOG FARM

You'll find a rainbow of colorful items at the Double Stink Hog Farm, located outside of Georgetown: geraniums, petunias, sweet corn, tomatoes, pumpkins, Indian corn and corn shocks. The farm, which once emphasized hog production, is a center for seasonal items from mid-April through Halloween. At the spring "Plowfest" you'll learn about plowing with teams of horses. In the fall you can pick the perfect pumpkin at the patch or farm market. During "Pumpkinfest" you'll also find horse-drawn wagon rides, grilled meats, fresh apple cider, pumpkin carving, farm animals, antique tractors, and craftspeople. During your visit, be sure to ask how this produce farm got its name.

PORK FAJITAS

2 pounds pork tenderloin	1 onion, sliced
3 tablespoons lime juice	1 green bell pepper, sliced
1/2 teaspoon coriander	8 flour tortillas
1/2 teaspoon chili powder	2 cups salsa
2 tablespoons vegetable oil	

Cut the pork into 1-inch strips. Place in a sealable plastic bag. Mix the lime juice, coriander and chili powder in a bowl. Pour over the pork and seal the bag. Marinate in the refrigerator for 3 hours. Drain the pork, discarding the marinade.

Heat the oil in a skillet or wok. Add the pork. Stir-fry for 4 to 5 minutes or until cooked through. Add the onion and bell pepper. Stir-fry until tender.

Microwave the tortillas on High for 50 seconds. Fill the tortillas with the pork mixture and use the salsa for dipping. *Yield: 8 servings.*

PORK FRIED RICE

1 1/2 tablespoons vegetable oil	1/2 cup sliced green onions including tops
2 eggs, beaten	
1 cup chopped cooked boneless pork	3 cups cooked rice, cooled
1 cup chopped fresh mushrooms	2 tablespoons soy sauce

Heat 1/2 tablespoon of the oil in a large skillet or wok over medium heat. Add the eggs. Cook until set; do not stir. Invert over a baking sheet to remove the eggs and cut into 1/2-inch strips. Heat the remaining oil in the skillet over medium-high heat. Add the pork, mushrooms and green onions. Stir-fry for 3 minutes or until tender. Stir in the cooked rice and egg strips. Sprinkle with the soy sauce and toss lightly. *Yield: 4 servings.*

BAKED STUFFED PORK CHOPS

1 cup chopped apples
1 1/2 cups bread crumbs, toasted
1/4 cup chopped onion
1/4 cup chopped celery
1 teaspoon salt
1/2 teaspoon pepper
1 tablespoon sugar
3 tablespoons milk
6 large pork chops with pockets
1/4 cup flour

Combine the apples, bread crumbs, onion, celery, salt, pepper and sugar in a bowl and toss to mix well. Add enough milk to moisten and mix well. Stuff into the pork chop pockets. Sprinkle with the flour. Place in a shallow 9×13-inch baking dish. Bake at 350 degrees for 1 1/2 hours, basting occasionally with the pan drippings. (If basting is not possible, you may bake covered and remove the cover during the last 30 minutes. If pork chops with pockets are not available, sandwich the apple stuffing between 2 thin pork chops.) *Yield: 6 servings.*

PORK CHOP BAKE

4 pork chops, 1 inch thick, trimmed
1/4 cup flour
2 teaspoons vegetable oil
2 (14-ounce) cans diced tomatoes or
   stewed tomatoes, cut up
Tomato juice
1 cup uncooked long grain rice
1 large green bell pepper, cut into
   strips
1 onion, chopped

Dredge the pork chops in the flour. Brown in the oil in a heavy skillet. Drain the tomatoes, reserving the juice. Add enough additional tomato juice to the reserved juice to measure 2 1/2 cups. Spread the rice in a 2 1/2-quart baking dish sprayed with nonstick cooking spray. Layer the pork chops, bell pepper, onion and tomatoes in the prepared dish. Pour the juice over the layers. Bake, covered, at 350 degrees for 1 hour. *Yield: 4 servings.*

The expression to "go whole hog" came from the eighteenth century when the English shilling was at one time called a "hog." Thus, a spendthrift, one willing to spend an entire shilling on the entertainment of a friend in a pub, was willing to "go whole hog."

WEST KENTUCKY-STYLE BARBECUED PORK CHOPS

$2^1/_2$ cups water
$^1/_4$ cup vinegar
3 tablespoons Worcestershire sauce
2 tablespoons butter
$^1/_4$ cup chopped onion
1 garlic clove, minced
1 tablespoon sugar
1 tablespoon salt

1 tablespoon black pepper
2 teaspoons chili powder
1 teaspoon red pepper
1 teaspoon red pepper sauce
1 teaspoon dry mustard
6 pork rib or loin chops, 1 to
$1^1/_2$ inches thick

Combine the water, vinegar, Worcestershire sauce, butter, onion, garlic,
sugar, salt, black pepper, chili powder, red pepper, red pepper sauce and dry
mustard in a 1-quart saucepan. Bring to a boil and reduce the heat. Simmer for
5 minutes. Pour into an airtight container. Chill, covered, for 8 to 12 hours to
allow the flavors to blend.

Reheat the barbecue sauce in a saucepan. Preheat the coals until ash gray in
color. Place the pork chops on a grill rack. Grill the pork chops for 12 to
15 minutes on each side or until cooked through, turning and basting frequently
with the barbecue sauce. *Yield: 6 servings.*

ORANGE PORK CHOPS

1 tablespoon vegetable oil
8 pork chops, $^1/_2$ inch thick
$1^1/_3$ cups uncooked instant
   rice

1 cup orange juice
Salt and pepper to taste
1 (10-ounce) can chicken and
   rice soup

Heat the oil in a large skillet over medium-high heat. Add the pork chops. Brown
quickly on both sides. Spread the rice in a 9×13-inch baking dish sprayed with
nonstick cooking spray. Pour the orange juice over the rice and mix well. Season
the pork chops with salt and pepper. Arrange over the rice mixture. Pour the soup
over the pork chops and cover with foil. Bake at 350 degrees for 45 minutes.
Bake, uncovered, for 10 minutes longer or until the pork chops are cooked
through. *Yield: 4 servings.*

PORK CHOP POTATO CASSEROLE

4 pork chops
5 medium potatoes, peeled and sliced
3 slices bacon
1 (10-ounce) can cream of mushroom soup
$^1/_2$ cup water
$^1/_2$ small onion, chopped
Salt and pepper to taste

Brown the pork chops in a nonstick skillet. Arrange the potatoes in an 8×8-inch
baking dish sprayed with nonstick cooking spray. Layer the bacon and pork
chops over the potatoes. Mix the soup, water and onion in a bowl. Pour over the
layers. Season with salt and pepper. Bake at 350 degrees for 1 hour.
Yield: 4 servings.

PORK CHOPS WITH WILD RICE

6 pork chops
1 cup uncooked wild rice
$1^1/_2$ cups water
2 cups undrained mushroom stems and pieces
1 tablespoon chicken bouillon granules
1 envelope dry onion soup mix
1 (10-ounce) can cream of mushroom soup

Brown the pork chops in a nonstick skillet. Line a 9×13-inch baking pan
with foil, leaving enough foil overhang to fold and seal. Spread the rice in the
prepared pan. Add the water and mushrooms. Sprinkle with the chicken
bouillon granules and dry onion soup mix. Layer $^1/_2$ of the soup, pork chops
and remaining soup over the layers. Fold the foil over the top and seal securely.
Bake at 325 degrees for $1^1/_2$ hours. *Yield: 6 servings.*

Sausage Blueberry Breakfast Cake

1 pound bulk pork sausage
2 cups flour
1 teaspoon baking powder
$^1/_2$ teaspoon baking soda
$^1/_2$ cup (1 stick) margarine, softened
$^3/_4$ cup sugar
$^1/_4$ cup packed brown sugar
2 eggs

1 cup sour cream
1 cup blueberries
$^1/_2$ cup pecans
$^1/_2$ cup sugar
2 tablespoons cornstarch
$^1/_2$ cup water
2 cups blueberries
$^1/_2$ teaspoon lemon juice

Brown the sausage in a skillet, stirring until crumbly; drain. Mix the flour, baking powder and baking soda together. Beat the margarine, $^3/_4$ cup sugar and brown sugar in a mixing bowl until light and fluffy. Add the eggs 1 at a time, beating for 1 minute after each addition. Add the flour mixture alternately with the sour cream, beating well after each addition. Fold in the sausage and 1 cup blueberries. Pour into an ungreased 9×13-inch baking pan. Sprinkle with the pecans. Bake at 350 degrees for 35 to 40 minutes.

Combine $^1/_2$ cup sugar and cornstarch in a saucepan. Add the water and 2 cups blueberries. Cook until bubbly, stirring frequently. Stir in the lemon juice. Spoon over the breakfast cake to serve. *Yield: 12 servings.*

Most farm families in the 1950s raised a few hogs for individual family use. Killing hogs, making sausage, rendering lard, and curing hams were typical annual food production activities.

Breakfast Soufflé

1 pound bulk pork sausage
8 eggs, beaten
2 cups milk
Salt to taste

1 teaspoon dry mustard
10 slices bread, cut into cubes
1 cup (4 ounces) shredded Cheddar
   cheese

Brown the sausage in a skillet, stirring until crumbly; drain and cool. Mix the eggs, milk, salt, dry mustard and bread in a large bowl. Fold in the sausage. Pour into a 9×13-inch baking dish. Chill, covered, for 8 to 12 hours. Sprinkle with the cheese. Bake at 350 degrees for 45 minutes or until set. Cut into squares to serve. *Yield: 12 servings.*

Goetta

1½ pounds bulk mild pork sausage
12 cups water (3 quarts)
1 (32-ounce) package pinhead oats
1 tablespoon salt

⅛ teaspoon pepper
1 onion, finely chopped
2 or 3 bay leaves
Vegetable oil for frying

Crumble the sausage into a 6-quart saucepan. Add the water, oats, salt, pepper, onion and bay leaves. Cook over low heat for ½ to 2 hours, stirring frequently. (The oats will absorb all of the water and the mixture will be very difficult to stir when the cooking is complete.) Discard the bay leaves. Pack into 3 large loaf pans. Chill in the refrigerator. To serve, cut the goetta into slices. Fry in a small amount of oil until crisp. (You may store in the refrigerator for several days or store in the freezer.) *Yield: 24 servings.*

Kentucky Culture

Goetta

Northern Kentucky, the home of many German immigrants beginning in the mid-1800s, is also the home of goetta, a dish with German roots. Although goetta recipes vary by family, it is a basic mixture of pork (with the possible addition of beef), cooked with pinhead oats. Pinhead oats are fine-ground oats. Goetta is cooked for several hours to mix and thicken, poured into loaf pans, and then cooled. Sliced goetta is fried until it is very brown and crunchy on the outside—the way most like it! It is traditionally a cold weather food, served at breakfast with eggs, but can be enjoyed any time of the day or year.

KENTUCKY SAUSAGE AND CORN CASSEROLE

1 pound bulk pork sausage
2 (8-ounce) cans cream-style corn
1 cup sour cream
1 (8½-ounce) package corn muffin mix
2 eggs, lightly beaten
1 onion, chopped
½ cup (1 stick) butter, melted
8 ounces Cheddar cheese, shredded

Brown the sausage in a skillet over medium heat, stirring until crumby; drain
on paper towels. Combine the corn, sour cream, corn muffin mix, eggs, onion,
butter and cheese in a large bowl and mix well. Stir in the drained sausage.
Spoon into a greased 9×13-inch baking dish. Bake at 350 degrees for
45 minutes or until cooked through. *Yield: 10 servings.*

PORK SAUSAGE RING

2 eggs, lightly beaten
½ cup milk
1½ cups cracker crumbs
¼ cup minced onion
1 cup chopped peeled cooking apple
2 pounds bulk pork sausage

Combine the eggs, milk, cracker crumbs, onion, apple and sausage in a
bowl and mix well. Press into a greased 6½-cup ring mold. Unmold onto a
10×15-inch baking pan. Bake at 350 degrees for 1 hour. Serve with scrambled
eggs in the center and garnish with sprigs of fresh parsley. *Yield: 8 servings.*

COUNTRY HAM

1 (16- to 20-pound) country ham
2 cups vinegar
1 cup orange juice
1 cup packed brown sugar
5 to 8 whole cloves
1 tablespoon allspice
1 tablespoon nutmeg
1/3 cup prepared mustard
1/2 cup packed brown sugar
1/2 cup carbonated beverage

Scrub the ham. Soak in cold water to cover in a large pan for 8 to 10 hours; drain. Place the ham in a 3- to 4-gallon stockpot and add enough water to cover. Add the vinegar, orange juice, 1 cup brown sugar, cloves, allspice and nutmeg. Bring to a boil and reduce the heat. Simmer for 20 minutes per pound. Turn off the heat. Let stand until cool. Discard the bones. Place on a large baking sheet. Mix the mustard, 1/2 cup brown sugar and carbonated beverage in a bowl. Spread over the ham. Bake at 400 degrees for 20 minutes. Cool completely before slicing. *Yield: 35 servings.*

KENTUCKY HAM SLICES

6 slices country ham, 1/2 inch thick (about 2 pounds)
2 cups packed light brown sugar

Trim any rind, fat and bone residue from the ham. Line a 9×13-inch baking dish with foil, leaving enough foil overhang to fold and seal. Sprinkle with a generous amount of the brown sugar. Alternate layers of the ham and remaining brown sugar in the prepared pan until all of the ingredients are used, ending with the brown sugar. Cover with the foil and seal. Bake at 325 degrees for 1 1/2 to 2 hours or until the ham is cooked through and tender. (This is a wonderful way to cook country ham for a large dinner party.) *Yield: 8 servings.*

Kentucky Culture

KENTUCKY COUNTRY HAM

Country ham is perhaps the most notable traditional Kentucky food. Recipes for the perfectly cured ham are often family secrets, but most involve salt (the basic curing ingredient), sugar (to enhance flavor and act as a softening agent), and saltpeter (a color fixing agent). When hams are taken out of the salt, they are dipped in boiling water and borax, dried and covered with a mixture of salt, red pepper, and saltpeter. They are then wrapped in brown paper, placed in a cloth sack, and hung in the smokehouse. To enhance their flavor, they hang through the month of June (called "going through the June sweat"). All hams must be washed off and soaked in water before cooking. Many Kentuckians wait one to two years for the best flavor before eating a ham.

COUNTRY HAM CHEESECAKE

Recipe courtesy of Sharon Thompson, Food Writer, *Lexington Herald-Leader*

1 cup potato sesame or butter cracker crumbs
1/2 cup grated Parmesan cheese
6 tablespoons butter, melted
1/2 teaspoon dill weed
4 ounces cream cheese with garlic and herbs, softened
4 ounces cream cheese, softened
3 tablespoons chopped chives
1/2 teaspoon dill weed
3 eggs
3/4 cup cream
4 ounces cooked country ham, grated

Combine the cracker crumbs, Parmesan cheese, butter and 1/2 teaspoon dill weed in a bowl and toss to mix well. Pat in a 9-inch springform pan. Bake at 350 degrees for 8 minutes. Cool slightly before filling. (You may prepare up to this point earlier in the day and store in the refrigerator until ready to add the filling.)

Beat the cream cheese with garlic and herbs, cream cheese, chives, 1/2 teaspoon dill weed, eggs and cream in a large bowl until smooth. Stir in the country ham. Spoon into the prepared crust. Bake at 350 degrees for 25 minutes or until the filling is set about 1 inch from the center. Remove from the oven to cool. Chill in the refrigerator until ready to serve. *Yield: 20 servings.*

HOMEGROWN PORK

Raising a few hogs on the small family farm ensured a good supply of pork chops, tenderloin, sausage, bacon, and ham for meals. Families or neighbors gathered on a bitter cold day to prepare the meat products. Each had their own special blend of seasonings for fresh sausage that was stuffed in muslin sausage sacks sewed by the women and girls. Some of the work crew gathered in the smokehouse to prepare the curing mixture for the hams. Others rendered the fat over huge outdoor kettles to make lard for use throughout the year. At the end of the workday everyone enjoyed a meal of fresh fried tenderloin served with crispy cracklin' corn bread.

COUNTRY HAM CUPS

2 cups ground cooked country ham
2 cups (8 ounces) shredded sharp
    Cheddar cheese
$^{1}/_{2}$ cup mayonnaise
24 slices white bread

Combine the ham, cheese and mayonnaise in a bowl and mix well, adding
additional mayonnaise if needed. Cut a circle from each slice of bread using a
biscuit cutter. Place between 2 sheets of waxed paper and flatten with a rolling
pin. Press into muffin cups sprayed with nonstick cooking spray. Bake at
375 degrees for 10 minutes or until light brown. Reduce the oven temperature
to 325 degrees. Fill each cup with the ham mixture. Bake for 15 minutes or until
the cheese is melted. Serve hot. *Yield: 24 servings.*

KENTUCKY HOT BROWN

Recipe courtesy of Rex Lyons, Chef, Kentucky Governor's Mansion, Frankfort

$^{1}/_{2}$ cup (1 stick) butter
3 tablespoons flour
2 cups milk
Tabasco sauce to taste
$^{1}/_{2}$ container grated Parmesan cheese
2 egg yolks
1 cup (4 ounces) shredded Colby
    cheese
1 cup (4 ounces) shredded American
    cheese
6 slices bread, toasted
6 slices cooked chicken or turkey
6 slices cooked country ham
2 tomatoes, sliced
12 slices bacon, cooked
Paprika to taste

Melt the butter in a 4-quart heavy saucepan. Stir in the flour until smooth. Add
the milk gradually, stirring constantly. Cook until thickened, stirring constantly.
Stir in Tabasco sauce and the Parmesan cheese. Remove from the heat. Stir $^{1}/_{2}$
cup of the sauce into the egg yolks. Stir the egg yolk mixture into the sauce. Cook
until thickened, stirring constantly. Stir in the Colby cheese and American cheese.
Remove from the heat. Cut each piece of toast in half and place on an ovenproof
plate. Layer each with the chicken, ham, sauce, tomatoes and 2 slices of bacon.
Sprinkle with paprika. Bake at 400 degrees for 10 to 15 minutes. *Yield: 6 servings.*

Slow-Cooked Fresh Ham with Dijon Chardonnay

Kentucky Fresh

Recipe courtesy of Ouita Michel, Chef/Owner, Holly Hill Inn, Midway

1 (7-pound) fresh ham or pork
    shoulder
2 tablespoons granulated garlic
2 tablespoons kosher salt
2 tablespoons freshly ground pepper

1/4 cup olive oil
2 cups Dijon mustard
2 sprigs of rosemary
1 bottle of Chardonnay or Riesling

Let the ham warm up a bit if possible. Mix the garlic, kosher salt and pepper together and rub over the ham to coat thoroughly. Brown the ham on all sides in the olive oil in a large roasting pan. Turn the ham fat side up and spread with the mustard. Add the rosemary and wine. Bake, covered, at 325 degrees for 2 1/2 to 3 hours or until a meat thermometer registers 165 degrees. Remove the ham to a serving platter, reserving the pan juices. Cut the ham into slices. Skim the pan juices and serve with the ham. *Yield: 12 servings.*

This dish is best baked in a large roasting pan with a tight-fitting lid—like a Dutch oven or in my case just a twenty-year-old hand-me-down pan from my mom. The pan needs to be able to hold the ham. I have used foil to cover, but the ham is not as tender.

Ham and Cheese Bundles

1 cup finely chopped cooked ham
1/2 cup (2 ounces) shredded Swiss
    cheese

1 1/2 tablespoons spicy brown mustard
1/8 teaspoon garlic powder
1 (8-count) can crescent rolls

Combine the ham, cheese, brown mustard and garlic powder in a bowl and mix well. Unroll the crescent roll dough and press the perforations to seal. Cut into 8 squares. Spoon about 1 tablespoon of the ham mixture evenly in the center of each square. Bring the corners to the center over the filling and twist and pinch the dough to seal. Arrange on a lightly greased baking sheet. Bake at 350 degrees for 15 to 18 minutes or until golden brown. *Yield: 8 servings.*

Breakfast Ham Casserole

3 cups French bread cubes
³/₄ cup chopped lean cooked ham
2 tablespoons chopped red bell
    pepper
1 cup (4 ounces) shredded reduced-
    fat sharp Cheddar cheese

1¹/₃ cups skim milk
³/₄ cup egg substitute
¹/₄ teaspoon dry mustard
¹/₄ teaspoon onion powder
¹/₄ teaspoon white pepper
¹/₈ teaspoon paprika

Place the bread evenly in an 8×8-inch baking dish sprayed with nonstick cooking spray. Layer the ham, bell pepper and cheese over the bread. Blend the milk, egg substitute, dry mustard, onion powder and white pepper in a bowl. Pour over the layers. Chill, covered, for 8 hours. Remove from the refrigerator and let stand for 30 minutes before baking. Bake, uncovered, at 350 degrees for 30 minutes. Sprinkle with the paprika. Serve immediately. *Yield: 6 servings.*

Ham and Sweet Potato Casserole

¹/₂ cup packed brown sugar
2¹/₂ cups flour
¹/₄ cup (¹/₂ stick) butter
2 cups sliced cooked sweet potatoes

2¹/₂ cups pineapple chunks
2 cups chopped cooked ham
¹/₂ cup pineapple juice

Mix the brown sugar and flour in a bowl. Cut in the butter until crumbly. Roll into a rectangle on a lightly floured surface. Layer the sweet potatoes, pineapple chunks and ham in a greased 2-quart baking dish. Arrange the pastry over the layers. Pour the pineapple juice over the top. Bake at 350 degrees for 1 hour. *Yield: 6 servings.*

Carving Pork

Carving pork is easy when you have the right tools and understand the technique. Make sure you have a sharp knife, a carving fork, and a cutting board. To carve a pork roast:

- *Remove the roast from the oven and let rest for 10 to 15 minutes.*
- *Look at which direction the muscle fibers run in the pork (this is called the grain).*
- *Hold the roast firmly in place with the carving fork and slice the roast across (at a right angle to) the grain.*

CHEF JIM'S FAMOUS PORK SANDWICH

Recipe courtesy of Jim Gerhardt, Chef, The Seelbach Hilton, Louisville

1 (14-pound) fresh ham, trimmed
1 garlic bulb, separated into cloves
    and peeled
6 tablespoons (3 ounces) extra-virgin
    olive oil
1 garlic bulb, minced
1 medium onion
1 bunch fresh cilantro
2 tablespoons cumin
1 teaspoon thyme
2 tablespoons black pepper
Juice of 3 limes
1 bunch fresh parsley

Salt to taste
6 tablespoons (3 ounces) white wine
    vinegar
2 serrano chiles, minced
$\frac{1}{4}$ cup (2 ounces) red wine vinegar
$\frac{1}{2}$ bunch fresh parsley, chopped
$\frac{1}{4}$ cup (2 ounces) caramel sugar
    syrup
$\frac{1}{4}$ teaspoon cayenne pepper
25 lettuce leaves
25 slices tomatoes
25 slices sweet onion
50 slices wheat or onion bread

Cut the ham with a paring knife every 4 inches and insert a whole garlic clove until the ham is completely studded with garlic. Process the olive oil, minced garlic, onion, cilantro, cumin, thyme, black pepper, lime juice, 1 bunch parsley and salt in a blender until smooth. Rub over the ham. Chill, covered, for 8 to 12 hours, rubbing occasionally. Place the ham in a roasting pan. Bake at 340 degrees for $3\frac{1}{2}$ hours or until a meat thermometer inserted in the center registers 160 degrees, basting with the pan juices every 30 minutes. Remove from the oven and let stand for 20 minutes before slicing.

Combine the white wine vinegar, serrano chiles, red wine vinegar, $\frac{1}{2}$ bunch parsley, caramel sugar syrup and cayenne pepper in a bowl and mix well.

To serve, cut the ham into thin slices. Layer the ham, 1 teaspoon of the sauce, lettuce, tomato and onion on $\frac{1}{2}$ of the bread slices. Top with the remaining bread slices. *Yield: 25 servings.*

The amazing utility of the hog has motivated the saying, "We use everything but the oink."

PREMIUM POULTRY AND EGGS
Chicken · Turkey · Eggs

Sponsor: Kentucky Poultry Federation / Kentucky Egg Council

PREMIUM POULTRY AND EGGS
Chicken • Turkey • Eggs

Poultry (broilers and eggs) is the second largest commodity in Kentucky, second only to horses. Kentucky is home to some of the most modern poultry facilities in the world. The leading companies in the poultry and egg industry all have operations in Kentucky: Tyson, Perdue, ConAgra, and Cagle-Keystone all produce broilers; Cal Maine produces eggs; and Cobb-Avian produces breeding stock within the Commonwealth.

The Kentucky Poultry Federation is a nonprofit organization that has been in existence since 1956. The Kentucky Poultry Federation and its egg promotion arm, the Kentucky Egg Council, promote chicken and egg products to consumers and the food service industry. The Kentucky Poultry Federation serves all the poultry industry on issues that impact poultry production throughout the Commonwealth.

Kentucky is the tenth largest state in broiler production. The broiler industry produces more than 253 million broilers, weighing a total of 1.3 billion pounds and valued at $504 million. Broiler companies operate five hatcheries in Kentucky. Each week, more than 6.6 million eggs are set in these hatcheries and 5.4 million broilers are placed in poultry houses on Kentucky farms. More than 700 Kentucky farm families in 40 counties raise poultry as part of their farming operation. Kentucky farmers produce enough chicken to feed over 12 million people.

Kentucky has always had a viable egg production industry. New operations and the expansion of existing operations have increased the value of egg production to $73 million annually. Kentucky produces over 933 million eggs yearly, which is equivalent to the egg consumption of more than 2.5 million people.

KENTUCKY ROSEMARY LEMON BAKED CHICKEN

1 (3- to 5-pound) chicken
3 tablespoons olive oil or vegetable oil
Salt and pepper to taste
2 tablespoons rosemary, or 6 tablespoons fresh rosemary
1 lemon, cut into halves
1 medium onion, cut into halves
1 tablespoon whole cloves
1 tablespoon flour or cornstarch
1 cup water
1 tablespoon butter

Rinse the chicken under cold water and pat dry with paper towels so the seasonings will adhere to the chicken. Rub with the olive oil, salt and pepper. Place the rosemary and lemon halves in the chicken cavity. Stud the onion halves with cloves and place in the chicken cavity. Place in a roasting pan. Bake, uncovered, at 375 degrees for 1 to 1½ hours or until a meat thermometer inserted into the thickest portion registers 190 degrees.

Drain the chicken, reserving 2 tablespoons of the pan juices. Mix the flour and water in a saucepan. Add the reserved pan juices. Bring to a boil, stirring constantly. Add salt, pepper and butter. Cook until thickened, stirring constantly. Strain the gravy through cheesecloth if desired. To serve, carve the chicken and serve with the gravy. *Yield: 4 servings.*

HERB-ROASTED CHICKEN AND POTATOES

4 medium baking potatoes (1½ pounds)
3 garlic cloves, finely chopped
1 tablespoon olive oil
1 tablespoon grated orange zest
1 tablespoon thyme
1 tablespoon oregano
2 teaspoons rosemary
1 teaspoon salt
1 teaspoon coarsely ground pepper
1 (3½-pound) chicken, cut into 8 pieces

Scrub the potatoes. Cut the unpeeled potatoes lengthwise into 8 pieces. Place in a large bowl. Combine the garlic, olive oil, orange zest, thyme, oregano, rosemary, salt and pepper in a small bowl and mix well. Pour ½ of the mixture over the potatoes and toss to coat.

Place the chicken in a large shallow roasting pan. Brush with the remaining garlic mixture. Arrange the coated potatoes around the chicken. Bake at 425 degrees for 45 minutes or until a meat thermometer inserted into the thickest portion of the chicken registers 180 degrees and the potatoes are fork-tender. (This recipe is easy to prepare, and the smell of the herbs is very stimulating to the appetite.) *Yield: 6 servings.*

Chicken and Corn Bread Dressing

1 (3- to 4-pound) hen
Salt to taste
$\frac{1}{4}$ cup vegetable oil
2 eggs
$1\frac{1}{2}$ cups buttermilk
2 cups cornmeal
8 biscuits, crumbled
$\frac{1}{2}$ to $\frac{3}{4}$ cup chopped onion
2 teaspoons poultry seasoning
2 eggs

Cook the hen in salted water to cover in a large stockpot until cooked through. Drain the hen, reserving 6 cups of the broth. Chop the hen, discarding the skin and bones.

Heat the oil in a cast-iron skillet in a preheated 425-degree oven. Beat 2 eggs and buttermilk in a large bowl until blended. Stir in the cornmeal. Add the hot oil from the skillet and mix well. Pour into the hot skillet. Bake at 425 degrees for 20 to 25 minutes or until golden brown. Invert onto a platter to cool.

Crumble the corn bread and biscuits into a large bowl. Add the onion, poultry seasoning, 2 eggs and reserved chicken broth and mix well. Let stand for 30 to 45 minutes, stirring occasionally. (The mixture should be the consistency of corn bread batter.)

Place the chopped hen in a large baking dish. Pour the corn bread mixture over the chicken. Bake at 400 degrees for 30 to 40 minutes or until brown. (The finished product should be soft but hold its shape.) Serve with giblet gravy if desired. *Yield: 15 servings.*

Keep Poultry Safe to Eat

Keep poultry separate from other foods in your grocery cart and in your refrigerator. Refrigerate poultry promptly after purchasing. Always thaw in the refrigerator, under cold running water, or in the microwave. Never thaw poultry at room temperature.

Always wash your hands before and after you handle uncooked poultry. Never place cooked poultry on a platter that previously held uncooked pieces of poultry. Always wash your knife and cutting board in hot soapy water before using again.

Use a clean meat thermometer to make sure poultry is cooked all the way through. Whole poultry pieces should be cooked to an internal temperature of 180 degrees. For turkey breast, cook to 170 degrees. Ground chicken and turkey should be cooked to 165 degrees. Refrigerate leftover poultry.

Loretta's Famous Chicken and Dumplin's

Recipe courtesy of Loretta Lynn, Country Music Legend,
Johnson County

1 (4-pound) hen
3 garlic cloves, minced
Salt and pepper to taste
3 cups flour
1 teaspoon salt
1 cup water
$1/2$ cup cream

Season the hen with the garlic, salt and pepper. Boil in water to cover in a large stockpot for 2 hours, adding additional water as needed. Remove the hen to a platter, reserving 6 to 8 cups of the broth in the stockpot. Cut the hen into pieces, leaving the bone.

Sift the flour and 1 teaspoon salt together. Add to the water in a bowl gradually, stirring to form a soft dough. Knead thoroughly on a lightly floured surface. Roll into a rectangle and cut into strips.

Return the reserved broth to a boil in the stockpot. Add the dough strips. Cook, covered, for 10 minutes. Add the cream and hen pieces. Simmer for 5 to 10 minutes longer. (You may add cornstarch to thicken if needed.)
Yield: 10 servings.

CROPPER CHICKEN

2 chicken leg quarters
4 chicken breasts
$^1/_2$ cup flour
$^1/_3$ cup vegetable oil
1 teaspoon salt
$^1/_4$ teaspoon pepper
1 (20-ounce) can sliced pineapple

1 cup sugar
2 tablespoons cornstarch
$^3/_4$ cup cider vinegar
1 tablespoon soy sauce
$^1/_4$ teaspoon ginger
1 chicken bouillon cube
1 orange, cut into $^1/_4$-inch circles

Coat the chicken with the flour. Brown the chicken in the oil in a large skillet.
Place in a shallow 9×13-inch roasting pan. Season with the salt and pepper.

Drain the pineapple, reserving the juice in a 2-cup measure. Add enough
water to measure 1$^1/_4$ cups. Combine with the sugar, cornstarch, vinegar, soy
sauce, ginger and bouillon cube in a saucepan. Bring to a boil, stirring
constantly. Boil for 2 minutes. Pour over the chicken. Bake, uncovered, at
350 degrees for 30 minutes. Add the pineapple slices and orange slices. Bake
for 30 minutes longer. Serve with hot cooked rice. *Yield: 6 servings.*

WORKING WOMAN'S CHICKEN POTPIE

2 refrigerator pie pastries
2 or 3 chicken breasts, cooked and
    chopped
1 (10-ounce) package frozen mixed
    vegetables, blanched

1 (10-ounce) can cream of potato
    soup
1 (10-ounce) can cream of chicken
    soup

Spray a 9-inch pie plate with nonstick cooking spray. Line the pie plate with
1 of the pie pastries. Combine the chicken, mixed vegetables, potato soup and
chicken soup in a large mixing bowl and mix well. Spoon into the prepared pie
plate. Cover with the remaining pie pastry, sealing and fluting the edge. Cut 2 to
4 vents in the top. Bake at 350 degrees for 5 minutes. Place strips of foil around
the outer edge to prevent overbrowning. Bake for 40 to 55 minutes or until
golden brown. *Yield: 8 servings.*

MARROWBONE BARBECUED CHICKEN BREASTS

$^1/_2$ cup flour
Salt and pepper to taste
4 large chicken breasts
$^1/_4$ cup vegetable oil
$^1/_4$ cup ($^1/_2$ stick) margarine
1 cup ketchup
$^1/_2$ cup water
$^1/_2$ cup sherry
2 tablespoons lemon juice
$^1/_3$ cup chopped onion
2 tablespoons brown sugar
2 tablespoons margarine
1 tablespoon Worcestershire sauce

Mix the flour, salt and pepper together. Dredge the chicken in the flour mixture. Heat the oil and $^1/_4$ cup margarine in a skillet. Add the chicken. Cook until light brown. Arrange in a lightly greased 8×8-inch baking dish.

Combine the ketchup, water, sherry, lemon juice, onion, brown sugar, 2 tablespoons margarine and Worcestershire sauce in a saucepan and mix well. Cook until heated through. Pour over the chicken. Bake, covered, at 325 degrees for 1$^1/_2$ hours or until the chicken is tender. *Yield: 4 servings.*

KENTUCKY BARBECUE CHICKEN

2¹/₂ cups water
¹/₄ cup vinegar
2 tablespoons butter
2 tablespoons Worcestershire sauce
1 tablespoon sugar
2¹/₂ teaspoons pepper
2¹/₂ teaspoons salt
1 teaspoon dry mustard
¹/₂ teaspoon Tabasco sauce
¹/₄ onion, chopped
1 garlic clove, minced
8 chicken breasts or 8 chicken leg quarters

Combine the water, vinegar, butter, Worcestershire sauce, sugar, pepper, salt, dry mustard, Tabasco sauce, onion and garlic in a small saucepan and mix well. Bring to a boil.

Place the chicken skin side up on a grill rack to seal in the juices. Grill for 5 to 10 minutes or until a meat thermometer registers 170 degrees, turning frequently with tongs to prevent burning and basting frequently with the hot sauce. (Do not use a fork to turn the chicken because the juices will be released and the finished product will be dry. Keep a spray bottle filled with water handy to use when a flame flares up. Also, remember that a tomato- or sugar-based sauce has a tendency to burn. When using chicken leg quarters, the chicken is cooked through when the drumstick will twist out of the thigh joint. There should not be any redness in the joints.) *Yield: 8 servings.*

Kentucky Culture

RAISING CHICKENS ON THE FAMILY FARM

Many farm families raised their own chickens to provide food for the family. Baby chickens were a popular mail order item, and their arrival in a large cardboard box with quarter-sized air holes was an exciting family event. The brooder house was equipped with lights to keep the baby chickens warm, and they were fed and watered with great care. When they reached maturity, it was time to process them for the freezer or a family meal with milk gravy, mashed potatoes, fresh green beans, and hot biscuits.

Buttermilk Pecan Chicken

$1/2$ cup (1 stick) margarine
1 cup buttermilk
1 egg, lightly beaten
1 cup flour
1 cup ground pecans
1 tablespoon paprika

1 tablespoon salt
$1/8$ teaspoon pepper
$1/4$ cup sesame seeds
8 chicken breasts
$1/4$ cup pecan halves

Melt the margarine in a shallow 2-quart baking dish. Beat the buttermilk and egg in a bowl. Mix the flour, ground pecans, paprika, salt, pepper and sesame seeds together. Dip the chicken in the buttermilk mixture and then in the flour mixture. Place skin side down in the margarine and then turn skin side up. Place pecan halves on each piece. Bake at 350 degrees for $1^{1}/_{4}$ hours. *Yield: 8 servings.*

Microwave Pineapple Chicken

2 boneless skinless chicken breasts
1 (8-ounce) can pineapple chunks
8 teaspoons cornstarch
1 teaspoon ginger

2 tablespoons soy sauce
$1/2$ cup apricot preserves
1 (11-ounce) can mandarin oranges, drained

Cut the chicken crosswise into $3/4$-inch strips. Drain the pineapple, reserving 2 tablespoons of the juice. Blend the cornstarch, ginger, reserved pineapple juice and soy sauce in a 2-quart microwave-safe dish. Stir in the preserves. Add the chicken strips and stir to coat. Cover with vented plastic wrap. Microwave on High for 4 minutes. Stir in the pineapple chunks. Microwave on High for 2 to 3 minutes or until the chicken is tender and cooked through, stirring once. Fold in the oranges. Cover and let stand for 2 minutes. Serve with hot cooked rice if desired. *Yield: 4 servings.*

ROLLED CHICKEN BREASTS

4 boneless chicken breasts
$^1/_4$ cup ($^1/_2$ stick) butter, softened
Salt and pepper to taste
2 teaspoons chopped fresh parsley
Canola oil for deep-frying
1 egg, beaten
$^1/_4$ cup milk
1 to $1^1/_2$ cups cracker meal

Pound each chicken breast skin side up to flatten. Mix the butter, salt, pepper and parsley in a bowl. Divide into 4 equal portions. Roll each portion into a ball. Place in the center of each chicken breast and roll up. Wrap in foil. Chill in the refrigerator.

Heat the canola oil in a deep fryer. Beat the egg and milk in a bowl. Roll the chicken in the cracker meal. Dip in the egg mixture and roll in the cracker meal again. Deep-fry for 15 minutes or until golden brown. (You may prepare ahead up to this point and freeze until ready to serve.) Place in a 12×12-inch baking dish. Bake at 350 degrees for 30 minutes. Garnish with fresh parsley. Serve with white sauce, cheese sauce or fruited salsa. *Yield: 4 servings.*

Make your own starter for white sauce by mixing 1 cup flour plus 1 cup margarine, softened, in a bowl until smooth. Spread in an ice cube tray or other shallow container and chill. Cut into 8 equal pieces. Freeze until firm. Place in sealable freezer bags. To make medium white sauce, use only 1 portion plus 2 cups cold milk. Heat until the sauce thickens, stirring constantly. A wire whisk helps make the white sauce smoother.

Chicken Broccoli Casserole

2 (10-ounce) packages frozen
    broccoli
4 to 6 cups 1-inch cooked chicken
    breast pieces
2 (10-ounce) cans cream of chicken
    soup

$^1/_2$ cup mayonnaise
1 teaspoon lemon juice
1 cup (4 ounces) shredded Cheddar
    cheese
$^1/_2$ cup cornflakes or bread crumbs
2 tablespoons butter, melted

Cook the broccoli using the package directions; drain. Spread the broccoli in a 9×13-inch baking dish. Layer the chicken over the broccoli. Mix the soup, mayonnaise and lemon juice in a bowl. Pour over the chicken. Sprinkle with the cheese. Toss the cornflakes with the melted butter. Sprinkle over the top. Bake, uncovered, at 350 degrees for 35 to 40 minutes. *Yield: 8 servings.*

Chicken Celery Casserole

8 boneless skinless chicken breasts
1 cup chopped celery
2 tablespoons chopped onion
1 (10-ounce) can cream of chicken
    soup

1 cup sour cream
1 cup crushed butter cracker crumbs
$^1/_2$ cup (1 stick) butter, melted

Place the chicken in water to cover in a saucepan. Bring to a boil over low heat. Cook until tender; drain. Cut the chicken into bite-size pieces. Combine the chicken, celery, onion, soup and sour cream in a bowl and mix well. Spoon into a greased 8×12-inch baking dish. Toss the cracker crumbs in the melted butter. Sprinkle over the chicken mixture. Bake at 350 degrees for 30 to 40 minutes or until golden brown. *Yield: 10 servings.*

POTLUCK PLEASING CHICKEN CASSEROLE

Kentucky Culture

4 chicken breasts
1¹/₂ cups water
1 tablespoon salt
1 (10-ounce) can cream of chicken soup
1 cup thinly sliced celery
¹/₂ cup cashews
³/₄ cup mayonnaise
3 hard-cooked eggs, coarsely chopped
2 tablespoons chopped onion
2 cups crushed potato chips

Cook the chicken in the water seasoned with salt in a saucepan until tender; drain. Cut the chicken into large chunks with scissors, discarding the skin and bones. Combine the chicken, soup, celery, cashews, mayonnaise, hard-cooked eggs and onion in a large bowl and mix well. Spoon into a 2-quart baking dish. Sprinkle with the potato chips. Bake, uncovered, at 450 degrees for 15 minutes. *Yield: 8 servings.*

ECONOMIC IMPACT OF THE POULTRY INDUSTRY

Each year the Kentucky poultry industry consumes twenty-four percent of the Kentucky corn crop and the equivalent of thirty-one percent of the soybeans. The investments of the poultry companies and Kentucky farmers into new facilities has allowed Kentucky's poultry industry to grow to twenty-seven percent of livestock cash receipts and seventeen percent of total agriculture receipts.

ALMOND CHICKEN FRANCAIS

8 ounces wide noodles
1 (16-ounce) package frozen French-
 style green beans
1 cup plain yogurt
1/2 cup lite mayonnaise
1/4 cup dry white wine
1/2 teaspoon parsley flakes
1 garlic clove, minced
1/2 teaspoon salt
1/2 teaspoon dill weed
1/8 teaspoon pepper
3 cups chopped cooked chicken
1 cup slivered almonds
1/3 cup grated Parmesan cheese

Cook the noodles using the package directions; drain. Cook the green beans
using the package directions; drain. Mix the yogurt, mayonnaise, wine, parsley
flakes, garlic, salt, dill weed and pepper in a bowl. Layer the noodles, green
beans, chicken, almonds, Parmesan cheese and yogurt mixture 1/2 at a time
in a 3-quart baking dish. Bake, covered, at 350 degrees for 45 minutes.
Yield: 8 servings.

*Feeding chickens was a daily chore on the family farm throughout Kentucky's history. In
addition to providing eggs and fresh poultry for the family, eggs were often sold to "city" folk
to provide extra income. Because caring for the chickens was generally a task for the mother,
she kept her "egg money" stashed away for emergencies or special occasions.*

HOOKTOWN HERB CHICKEN ALFREDO

1 pound chicken tenderloins
1/2 cup chopped sun-dried tomatoes,
    rehydrated
1 tablespoon chopped fresh basil
1 tablespoon chopped fresh
    oregano
1 cup freshly chopped portobello
    mushrooms
1 (8-ounce) jar Alfredo sauce
1 tablespoon chopped fresh oregano
2 tablespoons grated Parmesan
    cheese

Sear the chicken in a saucepan until cooked through. Remove the chicken and cut into large pieces. Return to the saucepan. Add the rehydrated sun-dried tomatoes, basil, 1 tablespoon oregano, portobello mushrooms and Alfredo sauce. Simmer over low heat for 10 minutes. Sprinkle with 1 tablespoon oregano and Parmesan cheese. Serve with hot cooked farfalle or bowtie pasta.
Yield: 4 servings.

HERBED CHICKEN PASTA

1 teaspoon vegetable oil
1 1/2 cups sliced mushrooms
1/2 cup chopped onion
1 garlic clove, minced
1 pound boneless skinless chicken
    breasts, cut into 1-inch pieces
1/2 teaspoon salt
1/2 teaspoon basil
1/4 teaspoon pepper
2 cups coarsely chopped tomatoes
4 cups hot cooked fettuccini (about 8
    ounces uncooked)
1/4 cup freshly grated Parmesan
    cheese

Heat the oil in a 10-inch nonstick skillet over medium-high heat. Add the mushrooms, onion and garlic. Sauté for 2 minutes. Add the chicken, salt, basil and pepper. Sauté for 5 minutes or until the chicken is cooked through. Add the tomatoes. Sauté for 2 minutes. Spoon over the hot cooked pasta. Sprinkle with the cheese. *Yield: 4 servings.*

CHICKEN TETRAZZINI

1 (10-ounce) can each cream of
    chicken and mushroom soup
1 cup chicken broth
2 cups grated processed cheese
6 cups cooked spaghetti
4 cups chopped cooked chicken

1 cup canned sliced mushrooms,
    drained
$1/2$ cup slivered almonds, toasted
$1/2$ cup grated Parmesan cheese
$1/2$ teaspoon paprika

Blend the soups and chicken broth in a large bowl. Stir in the processed cheese.
Add the spaghetti, chicken and mushrooms and toss to mix well. Spoon into a
7×11-inch shallow baking dish. Sprinkle with the almonds, Parmesan cheese
and paprika. Bake at 350 degrees for 30 minutes or until bubbly. (You may
substitute fresh mushrooms sautéed in 1 tablespoon vegetable oil for the canned
mushrooms.) *Yield: 6 servings.*

CURRIED CHICKEN PÂTÉ

1 medium onion, chopped
1 green apple, peeled and chopped
4 ounces slivered blanched almonds
$1/4$ cup ($1/2$ stick) butter
2 to 3 teaspoons curry powder
1 teaspoon salt

8 ounces cream cheese, softened
4 cups chopped cooked chicken
$1/4$ cup heavy cream
1 tablespoon chutney (optional)
2 green onions, sliced

Sauté the onion, apple and almonds in the butter in a saucepan over medium
heat until the onion and apple are tender. Add the curry powder and salt. Sauté
for 1 minute longer. Remove from the heat and cool slightly. Process the cream
cheese in a food processor fitted with a metal blade until light and fluffy. Add the
chicken, cream, chutney, sautéed apple mixture and green onions. Process until
smooth. Adjust the seasonings. Spoon into decorative crocks. Cover with plastic
wrap and chill. Serve with assorted crackers. *Yield: 64 servings.*

*Don't let the word "pâté" fool you. There is no liver in the recipe. The richness
of this smooth pâté comes from high-quality dairy and chicken products.*

Fruited Chicken Salad

5 cups cooked chicken chunks
2 tablespoons vegetable oil
2 tablespoons orange juice
2 tablespoons vinegar
1 teaspoon salt
3 cups cooked rice
1 1/2 cups small seedless green grapes
1 1/2 cups sliced celery
1 (15-ounce) can pineapple tidbits, drained
1 (11-ounce) can mandarin oranges, drained
1 cup slivered almonds, toasted
1 1/2 cups mayonnaise

Combine the chicken, oil, orange juice, vinegar and salt in a bowl and toss to mix well. Let stand for a few minutes. (You may chill, covered, at this point for 8 to 12 hours.) Add the rice, grapes, celery, pineapple, mandarin oranges, almonds and mayonnaise and toss to mix well. Serve on lettuce leaves.
Yield: 12 servings.

Lillian's Chicken Salad

6 boneless chicken breasts
1/2 cup water
1 (15-ounce) can pineapple tidbits, drained
1 1/2 cups seedless grape halves
1 cup chopped sweet pickles
1 cup chopped pecans
1 cup mayonnaise
Salt and pepper to taste
1 tablespoon lemon juice

Cook the chicken in the water in a slow cooker on High for 3 hours or until tender. Remove the chicken to cool. Cut into 1/2-inch pieces using scissors, discarding the skin. Combine the chicken, pineapple, grapes, pickles, pecans and mayonnaise in a large bowl and mix well. Season with salt and pepper. Sprinkle with the lemon juice. Chill, covered, until ready to serve.
Yield: 16 servings.

HOT CHICKEN SALAD

$1/3$ cup lite mayonnaise
1 teaspoon vinegar
$1/8$ teaspoon salt
$1/8$ teaspoon celery seeds
$1/8$ teaspoon pepper
1 cup chopped cooked chicken

$1/2$ cup chopped celery
2 tablespoons slivered almonds
1 teaspoon chopped onion
$1/2$ cup (2 ounces) shredded Cheddar
　　cheese

Blend the mayonnaise, vinegar, salt, celery seeds and pepper in a bowl. Combine the chicken, celery, almonds and onion in a bowl and toss to mix well. Add the mayonnaise mixture and toss to coat. Spoon into an 8×8-inch baking dish. Sprinkle with the cheese. Bake at 350 degrees for 20 minutes or until heated through. *Yield: 4 servings.*

HOT TURKEY SALAD

$1^1/2$ cups chopped cooked turkey
1 (10-ounce) can cream of chicken
　　soup
1 teaspoon lemon juice
$1/2$ cup cracker crumbs
1 cup chopped celery

$1/2$ cup mayonnaise
2 tablespoons dried onions
$1/2$ teaspoon pepper
3 hard-cooked eggs
1 cup Chinese noodles

Combine the turkey, soup, lemon juice, cracker crumbs, celery, mayonnaise, dried onions, pepper and hard-cooked eggs in a large bowl and toss to mix well. Spoon into a lightly greased $1^1/2$-quart baking dish. Sprinkle with the Chinese noodles. Bake at 350 degrees for 20 minutes. *Yield: 6 servings.*

Apple Cider Baked Turkey Breast

1 (5^1/$_2$-pound) turkey breast
1^1/$_2$ cups apple cider
^{1}/$_4$ cup soy sauce
2 tablespoons cornstarch
^{1}/$_2$ cup apple cider

Place the turkey skin side up in a large roasting pan. Bake at 450 degrees for 30 minutes or until the skin is crisp. Blend 1^1/$_2$ cups apple cider and soy sauce in a bowl. Pour over the turkey. Insert a meat thermometer into the thickest portion, making sure the meat thermometer does not touch the bone. Reduce the oven temperature to 325 degrees. Bake, covered, for 1^1/$_2$ hours or until the meat thermometer registers 170 degrees, basting frequently with the pan drippings. Mix the cornstarch and ^{1}/$_2$ cup apple cider in a bowl. Stir into the pan drippings. Return to the oven. Bake, uncovered, until the sauce is thickened. Serve the turkey with the sauce. *Yield: 8 servings.*

Miniature Turkey Meat Loaves

1^1/$_4$ pounds lean ground turkey
1 teaspoon Mrs. Dash seasoning
^{1}/$_2$ cup ketchup

Combine the turkey, seasoning and ^{1}/$_4$ cup of the ketchup in a bowl and mix well. Shape into 4 miniature loaves. Place in miniature loaf pans. Spread the remaining ketchup over the loaves. Bake at 350 degrees for 50 minutes or until cooked through. (This easy nutritious recipe was developed for the health-conscious person.) *Yield: 4 servings.*

Turkey Shiitake Burgers

3 ounces fresh shiitake mushrooms
1 small green bell pepper
1 small onion
2 tablespoons spicy steak sauce
2 tablespoons Worcestershire sauce
1 to 2 pounds ground turkey
Salt and pepper to taste

Process the mushrooms, bell pepper and onion in a food processor or blender until chopped. Combine the vegetable mixture, steak sauce, Worcestershire sauce, turkey, salt and pepper in a bowl and mix well. Shape into 4 patties or balls. Grill or pan-fry until the patties are cooked through. Serve on a toasted bun with lettuce, tomato and/or other condiments. *Yield: 4 servings.*

Compton's Mini Hot Browns

3 tablespoons margarine
3 tablespoons flour
$^1/_2$ cup (2 ounces) shredded sharp
   Cheddar cheese
1 cup milk
$^1/_2$ teaspoon salt
$^1/_2$ teaspoon white pepper
$1^1/_2$ cups finely chopped cooked
   turkey breast
8 slices bacon, cooked and crumbled
20 thin slices white bread
$^3/_4$ cup freshly grated Parmesan
   cheese

Melt the margarine in a medium saucepan over medium-low heat. Stir in the flour. Add the Cheddar cheese. Cook until the Cheddar cheese melts, stirring constantly. Increase the heat to medium. Stir in the milk gradually, whisking constantly. Cook for 4 to 5 minutes or until thickened and smooth, stirring constantly. Remove from the heat. Stir in the salt, white pepper, turkey and bacon.

Trim the crusts from the bread. Cut each slice into 4 squares and place on baking sheets. Broil until toasted. Spread a heaping tablespoon of the turkey mixture on the untoasted side of each piece of bread and return to the baking sheets. Sprinkle with the Parmesan cheese. Broil for a few seconds or until the Parmesan cheese melts and the topping is bubbly. *Yield: 80 servings.*

Morgan Cheese and Egg Salad Spread

2 cups (8 ounces) shredded processed cheese
4 hard-cooked eggs, chopped
$\frac{1}{2}$ cup mayonnaise or mayonnaise-type salad dressing
$\frac{1}{4}$ cup sweet pickle relish
1 teaspoon prepared mustard
Salt and pepper to taste

Combine the cheese, eggs, mayonnaise, pickle relish and mustard in a bowl and mix well. Season with salt and pepper. Serve on bread or crackers. *Yield: 6 servings.*

Eggs for a Crowd

18 eggs
1 cup sour cream
1 cup milk
2 teaspoons salt
$\frac{1}{4}$ cup ($\frac{1}{2}$ stick) margarine

Beat the eggs, sour cream, milk and salt in a mixing bowl until blended. Melt the margarine in a 9×13-inch baking dish, turning to coat the bottom of the dish. Pour the egg mixture into the melted butter. Bake at 375 degrees for 35 minutes or until set. *Yield: 12 servings.*

Pasta Vegetable Scramble

1/2 cup halved thin zucchini slices
2/3 cup chopped green onions with tops
1/3 cup julienned sweet red bell pepper
2 eggs
4 egg whites
2 tablespoons grated Parmesan cheese
1 tablespoon garlic salt
3/4 teaspoon Italian seasoning
1/8 teaspoon ground red pepper
4 ounces fettuccini or linguini, cooked and drained
4 cherry tomato halves

Spray a 10-inch omelet pan or skillet with nonstick cooking spray. Add the zucchini, green onions and bell pepper. Cook, covered, over medium heat for 3 minutes or until the zucchini is tender-crisp. Beat the eggs, egg whites, cheese, garlic salt, Italian seasoning and red pepper in a bowl until smooth. Pour over the vegetables. Add the pasta and tomatoes. Cook until the egg mixture begins to set, gently drawing an inverted pancake turner completely across the bottom and side of the pan. Continue cooking until the egg mixture is thickened but still moist. Do not stir constantly. Serve immediately. *Yield: 2 servings.*

Old-Time Lemon "Cheese Cake"

3½ cups flour
3½ teaspoons baking powder
¾ cup (1½ sticks) butter, softened
2 cups sugar
1 cup milk
1 teaspoon vanilla extract
6 egg whites, stiffly beaten
Lemon Icing (below)

Sift the flour and baking powder together 3 times. Cream the butter in a mixing bowl. Add the sugar and beat until light and fluffy. Add the flour mixture alternately with the milk and vanilla, beating well after each addition. Fold in the egg whites. Spoon into 3 greased and floured 8-inch cake pans. Bake at 375 degrees for 35 minutes. Cool in the pans for 10 minutes. Invert onto wire racks to cool completely. Spread Lemon Icing between the layers and over the top and side of the cake. (While the recipe does not contain cheese, it has been referred to as lemon cheese cake for generations.) *Yield: 8 servings.*

Lemon Icing

9 egg yolks
1½ cups sugar
1½ cups (3 sticks) butter
Juice and grated zest of 4 lemons

Mix the egg yolks, sugar, butter, lemon juice and lemon zest in a double boiler. Cook for 20 minutes or until thickened. *Yield: 8 servings.*

RIVERSIDE, THE FARNSLEY-MOREMEN LANDING

Step back in time with a visit to Riverside, a 300-acre nineteenth-century Ohio River farm. Just west of Louisville, this historic site features a two-story brick house with a reconstructed detached kitchen and kitchen garden. Sample the slower pace of nineteenth-century life by taking a seasonal riverboat excursion aboard the Spirit of Jefferson, a replica paddle wheeler. Special events, tours, and a museum store round out the offerings at this site dedicated to promoting and preserving historic farm life.

SAFE HOMEMADE ICE CREAM

Avoid homemade ice cream recipes that contain uncooked eggs. Uncooked eggs may contain salmonella bacteria that are commonly found in nature. With proper care and handling, eggs pose no greater food safety risk than any other perishable food.

Follow these simple steps to food safety when preparing homemade ice cream. Keep everything clean—freezer, dasher, storage container, and utensils. Cook the ice cream base over a low heat until a candy thermometer registers 160 degrees. After cooking, chill the base immediately and thoroughly before freezing. Pasteurized egg products that are available in grocery stores can be substituted for uncooked eggs in homemade ice cream.

WHITE CHOCOLATE LEMON MOUSSE PIE

1^1/$_2$ cups vanilla wafer crumbs (about 52 cookies)
7 tablespoons butter, melted
6 egg yolks
1 cup sugar
1 tablespoon grated lemon zest
^{1}/$_2$ cup fresh lemon juice
6 tablespoons butter, melted
^{1}/$_8$ teaspoon salt
3 ounces white chocolate
1^3/$_4$ cups heavy cream

Mix the vanilla wafer crumbs and 7 tablespoons butter in a bowl. Press into a 9-inch deep-dish pie plate. Freeze for 15 minutes. Bake at 350 degrees for 12 to 15 minutes. Cool completely.

Combine the egg yolks and sugar in a saucepan and mix well. Stir in the lemon zest, lemon juice, 6 tablespoons butter and salt. Cook over medium heat until thickened, stirring constantly. Do not boil or it will curdle. Remove from the heat. Let cool for 5 minutes. Add the white chocolate and stir until melted. Let stand until cool.

Beat the cream in a mixing bowl until stiff peaks form. Fold into the cooled lemon mixture. Pour into the prepared pie plate. Chill, covered, for 2 hours or up to 2 days. Garnish with whipped cream, chocolate leaves or a lemon twist. *Yield: 8 servings.*

Egg Custard Pie

3 eggs
$^1/_2$ cup (1 stick) margarine or butter, softened
$^1/_4$ cup milk
1 cup sugar
1 tablespoon flour
1 unbaked (9-inch) pie shell

Combine the eggs, margarine, milk, sugar and flour in a bowl and beat until smooth. Pour into the pie shell. Bake at 350 degrees for 30 minutes or until the crust is brown. *Yield: 8 servings.*

Sawdust Pie

Kentucky Fresh

Recipe courtesy of Patti's 1880s Restaurant, Grand Rivers

7 egg whites
$1^1/_2$ cups sugar
$1^1/_2$ cups graham cracker crumbs
$1^1/_2$ cups chopped pecans
$1^1/_2$ cups flaked coconut
1 unbaked (9-inch) pie shell
2 bananas, sliced
1 cup whipping cream, whipped

Combine the egg whites, sugar, graham cracker crumbs, pecans and coconut in a bowl and mix well. Pour into the pie shell. Bake at 325 degrees for 25 to 30 minutes or until glossy and set. Do not overbake. The center should be gooey. Cut into wedges while still warm and top with the bananas and whipped cream. *Yield: 8 servings.*

MAYSVILLE'S TRANSPARENT PIES AND TARTS

Transparent pies have been a favorite dessert since before refrigeration and preservatives. All one needed was milk, butter from the cow, eggs from the henhouse, sugar from the cane, flour from the grain, and a little salt to make these delicious confections. Local bakers keep this tradition alive, making Maysville the only area to market transparent pies and tarts in the United States.

Actor George Clooney, a native of Augusta, Kentucky, not only travels to Maysville to purchase transparent tarts, but has brought them to share at movie sets and television studios.

MAYSVILLE'S HISTORIC TRANSPARENT PIE

$^1/_2$ cup (1 stick) butter, melted
2 cups sugar
1 cup cream
4 eggs, beaten
2 tablespoons flour
1 teaspoon vanilla extract
1 unbaked (9-inch) pie shell

Beat the butter and sugar in a mixing bowl. Add the cream and mix well. Beat in the eggs. Stir in the flour and vanilla. Pour into the pie shell. Bake at 375 degrees for 40 minutes or until golden brown. *Yield: 8 servings.*

NO-WEEP MERINGUE

$^1/_2$ cup water
$^1/_4$ cup sugar
1 tablespoon cornstarch
$^1/_8$ teaspoon salt
3 egg whites

Combine the water, sugar, cornstarch and salt in a heavy saucepan. Cook over low heat until thickened, stirring constantly. Remove from the heat to cool. Beat the egg whites in a mixing bowl until stiff peaks form. Add the syrup in a steady stream, beating constantly. Spread the meringue over the top of your favorite pie. Bake at 350 degrees for 12 to 15 minutes or until the meringue is golden brown. (The meringue will not weep when served.) *Yield: 8 servings.*

KENTUCKY'S RURAL HERITAGE
Organizations Contributing to Our Development

In the early twentieth century, before good roads and automobiles were common, County Extension Agents were provided a mule allowance for travel. These two agents traveled mountain paths and winding roads to make home visits demonstrating and teaching various life skills to families in Harlan County in 1921.

Kentucky Farm Bureau

This Farm Bureau display at the 1951 Kentucky State Fair shows the amount of food that could be purchased with an average wage from one hour of labor in 1919, 1929, and 1951. The message: food was getting better and less expensive over the three decades that the chart represents.

Problem solving has been Farm Bureau's prime mission since its inception in 1919. Countless times over the past eighty-three years, Farm Bureau leaders have gathered around tables large and small to discuss their challenges and craft solutions. But in virtually all cases, before those assembled farmers could serve up a strategy for winning the next legislative battle, they served up a good meal of basic farm-grown food to fuel their creative energies. It should come as no surprise that food has been the first course at most Farm Bureau gatherings. After all, food is the farmer's business. Who could be in a better position to appreciate good cuisine?

Sometimes the food fare comes in the potluck category, with attending families each contributing a covered dish to supplement the main course. Other times, the food is all purchased, maybe from a caterer or the restaurant hosting the meeting.

In the 1930s and '40s, when county Farm Bureaus were getting organized and growing, their annual picnics served as a combined social occasion, business meeting, and member recruitment opportunity. On July 14, 1937, the Hickman County Farm Bureau hosted a massive gathering of farmers and family members totaling 3,000 people at the Columbus-Belmont Park on the Mississippi River. The menu that day was barbecue and fish.

Similar picnic programs that summer drew 1,000 folks to LaCenter and 600 to Burna in Livingston County. Two years later, in July 1939, the Crittenden County Farm Bureau hosted a barbecue for 400, with an unusual twist—a rolling pin throwing contest for ladies only. The winner was Mrs. I. W. Cook, who hurled her rolling pin 71.5 feet. Her skill and familiarity with the item suggests that homemade bread and pie crusts were routine staples on her family's kitchen table.

From those early picnics right on through the present, Farm Bureau functions have continued to be centered around breakfasts, luncheons, or dinners, and several service programs have emphasized the food connection as well. One very successful Farm Bureau event, the annual Kentucky Country Ham Breakfast at the State Fair, promotes one of the state's most unique and treasured food products and has raised more than $1 million for charity through the Grand Champion ham auctions. The first breakfast was held in 1964.

In the 1970s, Farm Bureau worked to improve demand for meat products, selling meat gift certificates during the Christmas season that could be redeemed at participating groceries. During the same period, Christmas citrus and nut products were first offered to Kentucky Farm Bureau members, shipped by truck directly from the Florida groves and processors. That program continues today, each December bringing around twenty tractor-trailers of the items to drop points all around Kentucky.

In the gourmet category, Farm Bureau sponsors an annual event on the Louisville Riverfront called the Ohio River Harvest Festival. The one-day program links area farmers with top chefs from Louisville restaurants, offering unique food items in sample-size portions for sale to visitors. The idea is to develop new markets for innovative food producers, emphasizing the freshness and quality that locally produced staples "bring to the plate."

From 1919 right on through the present, Farm Bureau leaders have never had a problem making the "farm to table" connection. Whether it's through tradition or outright necessity, they simply refuse, in most cases, to conduct business on an empty stomach. It seems when it comes to food, Farm Bureau members are their own best customers.

KENTUCKY ASSOCIATION OF ELECTRIC COOPERATIVES, INC.

Rural Electric official Claude Wickard addressed a 1947 picnic at Lincoln Memorial Park in LaRue County that drew 4,000 people from Southern and Central Kentucky. It was a combination fish fry and farm policy speaking event, and was a July 4th fixture for a number of years. Sponsors were the Hardin and LaRue County Farm Bureaus, the local REA, and Kentucky Farm Bureau.

Some sixty years ago, rural residents in Kentucky, and the nation, decided they wanted electric lines strung to their homes like people had in the cities. But, investor-owned utilities didn't think it was economically feasible to bring electricity to the countryside. So, farmers banded together and formed rural electric cooperatives. With the creation of the Rural Electrification Administration by President Franklin D. Roosevelt in 1935, the federal government began loaning money to help establish electric cooperatives. Electricity spread to every hill, hollow, and farm and greatly impacted the development of rural communities and the lifestyle of farm families.

In 1948, the then Kentucky Rural Electric Cooperative Corporation opened its doors in Louisville, Kentucky, to provide combined services for Kentucky's rural electric cooperatives. Even though over the years some of the services have changed—as well as the company name to Kentucky Association of Electric Cooperatives—that's still what they do today for the twenty-six electric co-ops they represent.

KENTUCKY EXTENSION HOMEMAKERS ASSOCIATION

This group of Kentucky Extension Homemakers members is dressed in their best as they prepare to travel to a mid-1930s Homemakers' conference. Homemakers continue to hold annual conferences at the county, area, and state levels to provide educational and leadership opportunities.

The Kentucky Extension Homemakers Association (KEHA) has roots that date back to 1912, when the University of Kentucky College of Agriculture made contacts with farm women using a demonstration train carrying a staff of lecturers and demonstration materials. Then, moveable schools, usually of three or four days' duration, were used to teach topics such as food preservation, clothing conservation, health, and sanitation. The work expanded when Home Demonstration Agents were hired in twelve counties, sometimes on a short-term basis.

By 1924, Home Demonstration Clubs were established to organize farm women for homemakers' work. In 1932 a state organization known as the Kentucky Federation of Homemakers was formed to unify the efforts of homemakers in Kentucky. In 1968, the name was changed to Kentucky Extension Homemakers Association.

Through the years, KEHA has met the challenges of developing new ideas and expanding programs to meet the changing needs of people. The organization of 27,000 members maintains their partnership with the University of Kentucky and Kentucky State University Cooperative Extension Service. Family and Consumer Sciences Agents serve as advisors to Extension Homemakers Clubs and provide research-based educational information for their programs. KEHA continues to be an effective way to develop leadership, promote volunteerism, and teach skills that members use to build strong families and communities through programs, projects, and activities.

COOPERATIVE EXTENSION SERVICE
"Serving Kentuckians in Every County"

Kentucky Cooperative Extension Service offices are a source of research-based information in agriculture, family and consumer sciences, youth development, and community resource development. Research is continually being conducted by faculty and staff from the University of Kentucky and Kentucky State University. We grow ideas that make a difference in your life, your family, and your community. From managing your money and your time to managing your crops and your livestock, from identifying the weeds in your yard to figuring out what makes your teenager tick, we are there to answer your questions. Please contact your County Extension Office for the most up-to-date information. Look for us in the phone book or on the web: www.ca.uky.edu.

4-H food demonstrations are a long-standing tradition in Kentucky. These young ladies were sure to have won a blue ribbon for their foods project work.

Kentucky homemakers could find a great deal of useful information from the Cooperative Extension Service to enable them to prepare nutritious and safe food for their families. From publications to demonstrations to educational meetings, a variety of resources were available from the University of Kentucky. Those services are still offered through County Extension Offices located in each county across the Commonwealth.

WEST KENTUCKY CORPORATION

West Kentucky Corporation is "Helping Make Things Happen" across the forty-five counties that make up the corporation. Established by the Kentucky Legislature in 1992, the corporation serves as a catalyst for creating higher-quality opportunities and an enhanced quality of life for the people across the western part of the state. By partnering with other community, state, and national business and public sector groups, the corporation works to build, expand, and sustain a powerful, globally competitive economy for Kentucky.

One of the goals of West Kentucky Corporation is to "foster the development of agriculture; natural, cultural, and tourism resources; and the strength of West Kentucky heritage to ensure long-term productivity and quality of life."

West Kentucky Corporation has been a leader in exploring diversification enterprises and value-added agriculture opportunities in the region. The development of an agri-tourism web page includes listings for individual businesses and information on area and regional agri-tourism venues such as barn tours. Another major initiative focuses on the development of regional Farmers' Markets. In cooperation with the Kentucky Department of Agriculture and Kentucky Farm Bureau, the corporation promoted agriculture by sponsoring an agriculture photo contest that received over 700 entries. They have sponsored Taste of Kentucky events at area "farm to table" programs and supported various agriculture conferences and programs throughout the region. The newsletters and web pages of the corporation are a source of up-to-date information on legislative issues and events related to agriculture.

The role of West Kentucky Corporation in developing our rural culture might best be summarized in the Annual Report statement of the Board Chairman: "While some people talk of success, we at West Kentucky Corporation will work hard to obtain success and with your continued support we will shape a brighter future for our region."

SPECIALTY SHOWCASE
Freshwater Shrimp · Fish · Lamb · Goat · Rabbit

SPECIALTY SHOWCASE
Freshwater Shrimp · Fish · Lamb · Goat · Rabbit

There are several farming enterprises in Kentucky that have developed or expanded in response to the changes in the tobacco industry. As a result, products such as freshwater shrimp, fish, lamb, goat, bison, and even rabbit are now being produced across the state.

The aquaculture industry has grown significantly, with over 500 acres in production annually. Catfish production is concentrated in the western part of the state, where 1.9 million pounds are produced. Over 100,000 pounds of freshwater shrimp, or more properly freshwater prawn, and 750,000 pounds of trout are produced annually throughout the state. Other aquaculture enterprises include black bass and paddlefish production.

Meat goats are considered to be one of the fastest growing livestock industries, with an estimated $30 million in returns to the Commonwealth. Goat meat, known as chevon, is the most frequently consumed meat in the world, and it is growing in demand because it is considered a high-quality protein, low in saturated fat and cholesterol. Sheep generate 1.25 to 1.5 million dollars per year in Kentucky. The numbers are stabilized in the state, with production concentrated in the central counties.

Bison, rabbit, and other specialty meats are not a large percentage of Kentucky's livestock industry, but they do provide income for many producers. They also provide variety and high-quality nutrition to family meals.

SHRIMP SCAMPI

1/2 cup (1 stick) margarine
1 tablespoon parsley
2 tablespoons lemon juice
1/2 teaspoon garlic powder, or 1 large
    garlic clove, minced

1/2 teaspoon salt
1 pound large fresh water shrimp,
    peeled with tails intact
1/2 teaspoon paprika (optional)

Place the margarine in a 2-quart microwave-safe dish. Microwave on High for
1 to 2 minutes or until melted. Stir in the parsley, lemon juice, garlic powder and
salt. Add the shrimp and toss to coat. Microwave, covered, on High for 3 1/2 to
5 1/2 minutes or until the shrimp turn pink and are tender, stirring twice. Sprinkle
with the paprika. (When using extra large shrimp, microwave for about 2 minutes
longer. Do not overcook or the shrimp will be tough.) *Yield: 3 servings.*

MONTGOMERY COUNTY LEMON SHRIMP

1 pound fresh water shrimp, peeled
    and deveined
5 ounces fresh mushrooms, sliced (2
    cups)
1 medium green bell pepper, cut into
    strips
1 1/2 cups bias-sliced celery
1/4 cup sliced green onions
2 tablespoons vegetable oil

1 (6-ounce) package frozen pea pods
2 tablespoons cornstarch
1 teaspoon sugar
1 teaspoon salt
1 teaspoon chicken bouillon granules
1/8 teaspoon pepper
1 cup water
1/2 teaspoon grated lemon zest
3 tablespoons lemon juice

Sauté the shrimp, mushrooms, bell pepper, celery and green onions in the hot
oil in a large skillet for 5 to 6 minutes. Add the pea pods. Sauté for 1 to 2 minutes.
Combine the cornstarch, sugar, salt, bouillon and pepper in a bowl. Stir in the
water, lemon zest and lemon juice. Stir into the shrimp mixture. Cook until
thickened, stirring constantly. Serve over hot cooked rice. *Yield: 4 servings.*

Fresh Water Shrimp on a Sweet Potato Bed

10 large fresh water shrimp
1 sweet potato, cooked
1 teaspoon cinnamon
1 teaspoon ground cloves
1 teaspoon ground nutmeg
2 tablespoons brown sugar
2 tablespoons honey
1/4 cup milk
1 cup flour
2 tablespoons butter

1 small yellow squash
2 ribs celery
2 tablespoons butter
1/4 teaspoon garlic salt
1/4 teaspoon pepper
2 tablespoons paprika
2 tablespoons marjoram
1/4 teaspoon garlic powder
1/4 cup (1/2 stick) butter, melted
6 tablespoons honey

Peel, devein and butterfly the shrimp. Chill in the refrigerator until ready to cook. Mash the sweet potato in a bowl until smooth. Add the cinnamon, cloves, nutmeg, brown sugar, 2 tablespoons honey, milk and 1/2 cup of the flour and mix well. Add enough of the remaining flour until the mixture is firm enough to hold its shape. Roll into balls using a number 24 scoop. Roll in the remaining flour to coat. Melt 2 tablespoons butter in a sauté pan. Add the sweet potato balls. Flatten each with a turner. Cook over medium heat until golden brown on both sides. Remove to a platter and keep warm.

Cut the squash and celery into short julienne strips, reserving the tops of the celery for garnish. Melt 2 tablespoons butter in a sauté pan. Add the squash and celery. Sauté until tender-crisp. Season with the garlic salt and pepper. Remove to a platter and keep warm.

Mix the paprika, marjoram and garlic powder in a small bowl. Sprinkle over the shrimp. Sauté the shrimp in 1/4 cup melted butter in a sauté pan until the shrimp turn pink. (The shrimp will have a few markings from the sauté pan on them.)

To serve, heat 6 tablespoons honey in a small saucepan. Place a sweet potato pancake on each serving plate. Arrange the sautéed vegetables on top to resemble a nest. Dip the shrimp in the heated honey and place 2 shrimp atop each vegetable nest. Garnish with the reserved celery tops. *Yield: 5 servings.*

SHRIMP CASSEROLE

1 cup uncooked rice
1 medium green bell pepper,
    chopped
1/2 small onion, finely chopped
1 (8-ounce) can sliced mushrooms,
    drained
2 tablespoons butter, melted
1 teaspoon seasoning salt or garlic

1/2 teaspoon pepper
1 (10-ounce) can cream of
    shrimp soup
1 pound fresh water shrimp or frozen
    shrimp, peeled and deveined
4 slices processed cheese or
    Cheddar cheese

Cook the rice using the package directions. Sauté the bell pepper, onion and mushrooms in the butter in a large skillet. Add the seasoning salt, pepper, soup and shrimp. Spoon into a greased 8×8-inch baking dish. Bake at 375 degrees for 15 minutes or until hot and bubbly. Sprinkle with the cheese. Bake for 5 minutes or until the cheese begins to melt. *Yield: 6 servings.*

COOKING FRESH WATER SHRIMP

Kentucky fresh water shrimp (prawns) should be kept refrigerated—preferably on crushed ice. Use them immediately. Rinse the shrimp in cold water just before cooking to remove any sediment. Shrimp are transparent and gelatinous when uncooked. When shrimp are properly cooked (approximately 2 to 3 minutes) depending on size, they become firm and opaque, appearing white, dappled with pink. Overcooking shrimp causes them to become tough.

In the early years of 4-H, cooking and canning clubs were popular among young girls. 4-H members from the Chevrolet community in Harlan County are ready to learn cooking skills at this 1922 4-H Food Club meeting. Food preparation and food preservation, along with a multitude of other projects, teach 4-H members "to make the best better."

Nuevo Latino Shrimp and Grits

Recipe courtesy of Anthony Lamas, Chef, Jicama Grill, Louisville

Juice of 1 lemon
1 tablespoon freshly chopped garlic
1 teaspoon oregano
1 teaspoon white pepper
1 teaspoon crushed red pepper
1 tablespoon kosher salt
1/4 cup olive oil
3 pounds Kentucky fresh water prawns, rinsed, peeled and deveined
Smoked Cheddar Chipotle Sweet Corn Grit Cake (page 85)
Oven-Roasted Onion and Tomato Salsa (page 85)

Whisk the lemon juice, garlic, oregano, white pepper, red pepper, kosher salt and olive oil in a bowl. Add the shrimp and toss to coat. Marinate, covered, in the refrigerator for 2 to 4 hours. Drain the shrimp, discarding the marinade. Arrange the shrimp on a grill rack. Grill for 2 1/2 to 3 minutes on each side or until the shrimp turn pink.

To assemble, place a Smoked Cheddar Chipotle Sweet Corn Grit Cake in the center of each serving plate. Spoon Oven-Roasted Onion and Tomato Salsa around the grit cake. Arrange 3 shrimp surrounding the grit cake with the tails facing toward the center. Garnish with fresh Silver Queen corn kernels and cilantro. *Yield: 10 servings.*

SMOKED CHEDDAR CHIPOTLE SWEET CORN GRIT CAKE

12 cups (3 quarts) water
1/4 cup olive oil
1 teaspoon kosher salt
1 (3-quart) container uncooked
    quick-cooking grits
1 cup (2 sticks) unsalted butter
1 (6-ounce) can chipotle chiles in
    adobo

2 pounds smoked Cheddar cheese,
    cut into 1-inch pieces
1 1/4 cups fresh Silver Queen corn
    kernels (about 4 cobs)
1/4 cup flour
Olive oil for frying

Bring the water, 1/4 cup olive oil and kosher salt to a boil in a large stockpot. Add the grits 1/4 cup at a time, whisking constantly. Cook until the mixture begins to thicken, whisking constantly. Add the butter and chiles in adobo. Cook for 2 minutes and reduce the heat. Add the cheese gradually, stirring constantly. Stir in the corn. Remove from the heat. Grease a half sheet pan with 1-inch sides with olive oil using a paper towel. Pour the grit mixture into the prepared pan, spreading evenly with a spatula. Cover with plastic wrap. Chill for 4 to 6 hours or up to 24 hours. (The mixture will coagulate.) Cut into desired shapes using a cookie cutter or cut into small triangles using a butter knife. Sprinkle with the flour. Fry in olive oil in a skillet for 2 minutes on each side or until golden brown. Arrange on a baking sheet. Bake at 350 degrees for 3 to 5 minutes. *Yield: 10 servings.*

OVEN-ROASTED ONION AND TOMATO SALSA

1 large Spanish onion, chopped
2 large Kentucky tomatoes, cut into
    halves
1 large jalapeño chile, chopped

Juice of 1 lime
1/4 cup olive oil
1 tablespoon kosher salt
1 bunch of cilantro, chopped

Combine the onion, tomatoes, jalapeño chile, lime juice, olive oil and kosher salt in a cast-iron skillet or heavy baking dish. Roast at 350 degrees for 10 minutes. Remove from the oven to cool. Pulse the tomato mixture and cilantro in a blender to create a chunky consistency. Pour into a bowl. Chill, covered, in the refrigerator. *Yield: 10 servings.*

FANCY FARM PICNIC

Summer time means picnic time and there is no picnic more famous than the one at Fancy Farm, held annually in Graves County since the 1800s. The event serves up pork and mutton barbecue with farm fresh vegetables and political speeches for dessert. Politicians from across the Commonwealth brave the hot steamy weather to speak to the citizens there. It is one of the largest political rallies in Kentucky, and the heated debates and hecklers' comments always produce a few statewide news stories.

Shrimp Pilau

1 pound uncooked shrimp, peeled
    and deveined
3 slices bacon, chopped
1 cup chopped green bell pepper
$^1/_4$ cup chopped onion
1 (16-ounce) can diced tomatoes

$^3/_4$ cup water
$^3/_4$ cup uncooked rice
1 teaspoon salt
$^1/_8$ teaspoon pepper
$^1/_8$ teaspoon thyme

Cut the shrimp into halves. Cook the bacon in a 2-quart saucepan until crisp.
Remove the bacon to paper towels to drain, reserving the drippings in the
saucepan. Sauté the bell pepper and onion in the reserved drippings until tender.
Add the tomatoes and water. Bring to a boil. Stir in the uncooked rice, salt,
pepper and thyme. Reduce the heat. Cook, covered, over low heat for 18 to
20 minutes. Stir in the shrimp. Cook, covered, for 10 to 12 minutes or until the
shrimp turn pink. Sprinkle with the bacon. *Yield: 6 servings.*

Sautéed Shrimp

8 ounces angel hair pasta
1 pound fresh water shrimp
$^1/_4$ cup (2 ounces) olive oil
1 teaspoon chopped garlic
2 tablespoons capers

$^1/_4$ cup (2 ounces) white wine
Juice of 2 lemons
2 cups heavy cream
1 teaspoon chopped parsley
Salt and white pepper to taste

Cook the pasta using the package directions; drain. Sauté the shrimp in the
olive oil in a heavy sauté pan for 2 minutes. Add the garlic and capers. Sauté
for 30 seconds. Add the white wine and lemon juice. Cook until the liquid is
reduced by half. Add the cream. Cook until the liquid is reduced by half.
Sprinkle with the parsley, salt and white pepper. Spoon over the pasta.
Yield: 4 servings.

SHRIMP CREOLE

½ cup chopped onion
½ cup chopped celery
1 garlic clove, minced
3 tablespoons vegetable oil
1 (16-ounce) can crushed tomatoes
1 (8-ounce) can tomato sauce
1½ teaspoons salt
1 teaspoon sugar

½ to 1 teaspoon chili powder
1 tablespoon Worcestershire sauce
⅜ teaspoon bottled hot pepper sauce
2 teaspoons cornstarch
1 tablespoon cold water
12 ounces uncooked shrimp, peeled
    and deveined
½ cup chopped green bell pepper

Sauté the onion, celery and garlic in the hot oil in a skillet until tender but not brown. Add the tomatoes, tomato sauce, salt, sugar, chili powder, Worcestershire sauce and hot pepper sauce. Simmer, uncovered, for 45 minutes. Mix the cornstarch with the cold water. Stir into the sauce. Cook until thickened and bubbly, stirring constantly. Add the shrimp and bell pepper. Simmer, covered, for 4 minutes or until the shrimp turn pink. Serve with hot cooked rice.
Yield: 6 servings.

GRILLED BLACK BASS WITH SESAME SEEDS

¼ cup vegetable oil
¼ cup sesame seeds
1½ tablespoons lemon juice

½ teaspoon salt
⅛ teaspoon pepper
6 pan-dressed black bass

Mix the oil, sesame seeds, lemon juice, salt and pepper in a bowl. Rinse the fish and pat dry. Place in well-greased hinged wire grills. Brush some of the sauce over the fish. Grill 4 inches from medium-hot coals for 5 to 8 minutes. Brush with the remaining sauce and turn. Grill for 5 to 8 minutes or until the fish flakes easily with a fork. *Yield: 6 servings.*

KENTUCKY AQUACULTURE ASSOCIATION

The Kentucky Aquaculture Association is a nonprofit member-based organization committed to the advancement of the aquaculture industry. Kentuckians consume an estimated 60 million pounds of seafood per year. This is worth approximately $68 million, but less than four percent is produced within the state. The Association works to obtain funding for aquaculture research and promotes sound economic and environmental practices. They work to increase aquaculture production and provide a marketing network for Kentucky-raised aquaculture products in the state as well as nationally and internationally.

TASTY CATFISH DIP

6 catfish fillets
6 ounces cream cheese, softened
1/3 cup chopped stuffed olives
1/4 cup mayonnaise or mayonnaise-
    type salad dressing
3 tablespoons half-and-half
1/4 teaspoon grated onion
1/4 teaspoon hot pepper sauce

Steam the fish in a steamer until white and flaky. (Do not let the fish touch the water.) Place the fish in a medium bowl and flake with a fork.

Combine the cream cheese, olives, mayonnaise, half-and-half, onion, hot pepper sauce and 1 cup of the flaked fish in a bowl and mix to form a paste. Spoon into a serving bowl. Sprinkle with the remaining flaked fish. Chill, covered, in the refrigerator. Garnish with chopped fresh parsley. Serve with potato chips and pretzel sticks. *Yield: 8 servings.*

BLACKENED CATFISH FILLETS

1 tablespoon paprika
2 1/2 teaspoons salt
1 teaspoon onion powder
1 teaspoon garlic powder
1 teaspoon cayenne pepper
3/4 teaspoon white pepper
3/4 teaspoon black pepper
1/2 teaspoon thyme
1/2 teaspoon oregano
4 farm-raised catfish fillets
1/2 cup (1 stick) unsalted butter,
    melted

Heat a large heavy skillet until very hot. Mix the paprika, salt, onion powder, garlic powder, cayenne pepper, white pepper, black pepper, thyme and oregano in a small bowl. Dip the fish in melted butter. Dredge in the seasoning mixture. Place in the hot skillet. Cook for 2 to 3 minutes on each side or until the fish is charred and flakes easily. Serve with a squeeze of fresh lemon. *Yield: 4 servings.*

CATFISH IN A BROWN BAG

4 or 5 catfish steaks, about 1 inch thick
Seasoned salt to taste
1/4 cup (1/2 stick) butter, melted
1 garlic clove, chopped
1 bunch scallions, cut into 1-inch pieces

8 ounces shiitake mushrooms, sliced
1/4 cup soy sauce
1/4 cup sherry
1/2 teaspoon ginger

Sprinkle the fish on all sides with seasoned salt. Mix the butter, garlic, scallions, mushrooms, soy sauce, sherry and ginger in a bowl. Place the fish in a nonrecycled brown paper bag and place in a shallow baking pan. Pour the mushroom mixture evenly over the fish. Pull the brown bag closely around the fish and seal the opening with string. Bake at 350 degrees for 30 to 35 minutes or until the fish flakes easily. *Yield: 6 servings.*

PURCHASE PAN-FRIED CATFISH

1/2 cup Weisenberger Mills Fish and Vegetable Batter Mix
1 teaspoon paprika
1/2 teaspoon each salt, celery salt and pepper

1/4 teaspoon dry mustard
1/4 teaspoon onion powder
1 pound catfish fillets
1 cup milk
2 tablespoons peanut oil

Mix the batter mix, paprika, salt, celery salt, pepper, dry mustard and onion powder in a shallow dish. Dip the fish in the milk. Roll in the seasoning mixture. Place in a single layer in hot peanut oil in a skillet. Fry over medium-high heat for 3 to 5 minutes or until light brown. Turn carefully. Fry for 3 to 5 minutes or until the fish are brown and flake easily with a fork. Remove to paper towels to drain. *Yield: 4 servings.*

For more information about Weisenberger Mills Fish and Vegetable Batter Mix, contact them at P. O. Box 215, Midway, Kentucky 40347, 1-800-643-8678 or at www.weisenberger.com.

SOUTHERN FRIED SPOONFISH

Recipe courtesy of Jim Gerhardt, Chef, The Seelbach Hilton, Louisville

8 plum tomatoes
1 pound spoonfish fillets
1/2 cup (4 ounces) buttermilk
1 cup flour
2 teaspoons salt
1 teaspoon pepper
1 teaspoon Cajun spice
Vegetable oil for deep-frying
1 cup tomato juice
Salt and pepper to taste
1 fennel bulb, julienned
1/2 onion, finely chopped
1/4 cup (2 ounces) olive oil
Juice of 1 lemon

Cut the tomatoes into halves. Place on a baking sheet. Bake at 350 degrees for 20 minutes or until roasted.

Soak the fish in the buttermilk in a bowl for at least 20 minutes. Mix the flour, 2 teaspoons salt, 1 teaspoon pepper and Cajun spice together. Drain the fish. Dredge the fish in the flour mixture twice. Deep-fry in the hot vegetable oil in a deep fryer until the fish is golden brown. Remove to paper towels to drain.

Purée 1/2 of the roasted tomatoes and tomato juice in a blender. Strain into a bowl, discarding the solids. Season with salt and pepper to taste.

Sauté the fennel and onion in the olive oil in a skillet until tender. Add the remaining roasted tomatoes. Season with salt and pepper to taste.

Serve the fish with the roasted tomato sauce and sautéed vegetables. Sprinkle with the lemon juice. *Yield: 4 servings.*

PARMESAN CATFISH

$^1/_2$ cup Italian bread crumbs
$^1/_2$ cup fine plain bread crumbs
$^1/_2$ cup grated Parmesan cheese
1 teaspoon salt
$^1/_2$ teaspoon pepper
$^1/_2$ teaspoon paprika

2 tablespoons chopped fresh parsley
$^1/_2$ teaspoon chopped fresh oregano
6 (8-ounce) catfish fillets
$^1/_2$ cup (1 stick) butter or margarine,
    melted

Mix the bread crumbs, Parmesan cheese, salt, pepper, paprika, parsley and
oregano in a shallow dish. Dip the fish in the butter. Dredge in the bread crumb
mixture. Place on a parchment-lined baking sheet. Bake at 375 degrees for
25 minutes or until the fish flakes easily with a fork. *Yield: 6 servings.*

TROUT WORCESTERSHIRE

2 pounds trout fillets
1 (10-ounce) can golden mushroom
    soup

2 teaspoons Worcestershire sauce
$^1/_4$ teaspoon thyme

Roll up the fish. Place in a well-buttered baking dish. Combine the soup,
Worcestershire sauce and thyme in a bowl and mix well. Pour over the fish.
Bake, uncovered, at 425 degrees for 20 minutes or until the fish flakes easily.
Garnish with parsley. Serve with lemon wedges, if desired. *Yield: 8 servings.*

LaRue Leg of Lamb

1 (6-pound) leg of lamb

1 (8-ounce) bottle teriyaki marinade

Place the lamb in a large sealable plastic bag. Add the marinade and seal the
bag. Marinate in the refrigerator for 8 to 12 hours. Drain the lamb, discarding
the marinade. Place on a rack in a roasting pan and cover with foil. Bake at 350
degrees for 1 hour. Bake, uncovered, for $1^1/_2$ hours longer or until the lamb
separates from the bone. *Yield: 11 servings.*

GRILLED LAMB CHOPS

Recipe courtesy of Angie Vives, Chef, Kentucky Lt. Governor's
Mansion, Frankfort

8 lamb loin chops, 1 inch thick
1/2 cup soy sauce
1/2 cup cider vinegar
3 garlic cloves, minced
2 teaspoons ginger

3 tablespoons honey
1/4 teaspoon dry mustard
1/4 teaspoon pepper
1/4 cup chopped fresh cilantro

Place the lamb chops in a shallow baking dish. Combine the soy sauce, cider
vinegar, garlic, ginger, honey, dry mustard, pepper and cilantro in a small bowl
and mix well. Pour over the lamb chops, turning to coat evenly. Marinate,
covered, for 8 to 12 hours. Drain the lamb chops, discarding the marinade.
Place the lamb chops on a grill rack. Grill for 8 to 10 minutes on each side or to
the desired degree of doneness. *Yield: 8 servings.*

GRILLED TERIYAKI LAMB CHOPS

4 (5-ounce) lean lamb chops, 1 1/2
   inches thick
1/2 cup chopped onion

1/2 cup reduced-sodium teriyaki sauce
1 teaspoon minced garlic

Trim the lamb chops. Place in a heavy-duty sealable plastic bag. Add the onion,
teriyaki sauce and garlic and seal the bag. Marinate in the refrigerator for
8 hours or longer, turning the bag occasionally. Drain the lamb chops, reserving
the marinade. Bring the reserved marinade to a boil in a small saucepan. Boil
for 3 minutes. Remove from the heat. Place the lamb chops on a grill rack
sprayed with nonstick cooking spray. Grill, covered, over medium-hot coals for 8
minutes on each side or until a meat thermometer registers 160 degrees for
medium or 170 degrees for well done, basting occasionally with the heated
marinade. *Yield: 4 servings.*

LAMB KABOBS

⅔ cup teriyaki sauce
3 tablespoons vegetable oil
2 tablespoons brown sugar
2 tablespoons finely chopped onion
2 teaspoons ginger

2 garlic cloves, finely chopped
4 lamb chops, cut into pieces
1 pound bacon, cut into pieces
1 (15-ounce) can pineapple chunks,
    drained

Combine the teriyaki sauce, oil, brown sugar, onion, ginger and garlic in a bowl and mix well. Place the lamb in a sealable plastic bag. Pour the marinade over the lamb and seal the bag. Marinate in the refrigerator for 3 to 12 hours. Drain the lamb, discarding the marinade.

Soak wooden skewers in water to cover for 1 hour to prevent burning. For each skewer, thread a piece of bacon on the skewer first. Then thread a piece of lamb, wrapping the bacon around the lamb. Next thread a piece of pineapple on the skewer. Repeat 1 to 2 more times depending on the length of the skewer. Repeat with the remaining skewers and ingredients.

Place the kabobs on a grill rack. Grill for 20 to 30 minutes or until the bacon is cooked through. Do not overcook. *Yield: 4 servings.*

MINTED LAMB LOAF

2½ pounds lean ground lamb
1 red onion, chopped
1 small green bell pepper, chopped
1 small red bell pepper, chopped
2 garlic cloves, minced
1 (8-ounce) can tomato sauce
½ cup fine dry bread crumbs
2 eggs, lightly beaten

½ cup loosely packed fresh mint
    leaves, finely chopped
2 teaspoons oregano
2 teaspoons basil
2 teaspoons pepper
1 teaspoon crushed rosemary
½ teaspoon salt

Combine the lamb, onion, bell peppers, garlic, tomato sauce, bread crumbs, eggs, mint, oregano, basil, pepper, rosemary and salt in a large bowl and mix well. Press into a greased 5×9-inch loaf pan. Bake, uncovered, at 350 degrees for 1½ hours or until cooked through. To serve, drain the juices and remove the loaf from the pan. *Yield: 10 servings.*

THE BARBECUE BY-WAY

To many people, the words "western Kentucky" and "barbecue" are synonymous. As you sample the delicious barbecue dishes of western Kentucky at festivals and local restaurants, you will find the secret is in the sauce. The barbecue dips and sauces vary from tomato-based to hot pepper and oil concoctions. Questions like, "Do you want your meat dipped or sprinkled?" show the diversity of this tasty tradition.

CHEVON KABOBS

1 chevon shoulder roast, cut into 1-
    inch cubes
$1/4$ cup vinegar
2 tablespoons olive oil
1 garlic clove, finely chopped

1 tablespoon sugar
$1/2$ teaspoon oregano
1 teaspoon salt
$1/4$ teaspoon pepper
4 small tomatoes, cut into quarters

Arrange the chevon in a shallow 9×13-inch baking dish. Combine the vinegar, olive oil, garlic, sugar, oregano, salt and pepper in a jar with a tight-fitting lid. Replace the lid and shake well. Pour over the chevon. Marinate, covered, in the refrigerator for 3 hours, turning occasionally. Drain the chevon, reserving the marinade. Thread the chevon and tomatoes alternately on skewers. Brush with some of the reserved marinade. Place the skewers on a grill rack. Grill 4 inches above the coals for 20 minutes or until cooked through, brushing several times with the remaining reserved marinade. *Yield: 12 servings.*

Goat meat is naturally low in saturated fat and calories. A 3-ounce portion of roasted goat meat contains 122 calories and 2.5 grams of fat, 7 grams of saturated fat, and 3.2 milligrams of iron.

BAKED RABBIT

1 rabbit, cut into pieces
1 envelope dry onion soup mix
1 (10-ounce) can fat-free cream of mushroom soup or
    cream of celery soup
$1^1/2$ cups water

Place the rabbit in a 2-quart roasting pan. Sprinkle the soup mix over the rabbit. Mix the mushroom soup and water in a bowl. Pour over the rabbit. Bake, covered, at 325 degrees for $2^1/2$ to 3 hours or until cooked through. *Yield: 4 servings.*

BARBECUED RABBIT

½ to 1 cup flour
1 teaspoon salt
½ teaspoon pepper
2½ pounds rabbit pieces
¼ to ½ cup lemon juice
2 to 4 tablespoons vegetable oil
¾ cup water
¼ cup plus 2 tablespoons chopped onion
1 tablespoon chopped green bell pepper

2 tablespoons butter
2 tablespoons brown sugar
2 tablespoons lemon juice
1 cup ketchup
1 cup water
1 teaspoon salt
1 teaspoon celery seeds
1 teaspoon dry mustard

Mix the flour, 1 teaspoon salt and pepper together. Brush the rabbit with ¼ to ½ cup lemon juice. Dredge in the flour mixture. Brown in the oil in a 10-inch skillet. Place in a 4-quart pressure cooker. Add ¾ cup water and ¼ cup onion and seal the pressure cooker. Pressure cook for 18 to 20 minutes using the manufacturer's directions. Brown 2 tablespoons onion and bell pepper in the butter in a 2-quart saucepan. Add the brown sugar, 2 tablespoons lemon juice, ketchup, 1 cup water, 1 teaspoon salt, celery seeds and dry mustard and mix well. Bring to a boil over high heat and reduce the heat. Simmer for 30 minutes. Add the rabbit. Simmer for 10 minutes. *Yield: 8 servings.*

WHERE THE BUFFALO ROAMED

For ten thousand years, since the end of the last ice age, buffalo made their home in Kentucky, displaced only when waves of settlers arrived.

When the large wooly mammals traversed the state, they created great highways in their wake. Buffalo roads were often several wagon widths wide with banks up to six feet high. They converged at wallowing grounds where the buffalo rolled in mud that caked onto their hides, discouraging biting insects.

Stamping Ground, Big Bone Lick State Park, and Blue Licks State Park have the conformation of a bowl carved by the wallowing buffalo. Today you can see the domesticated ancestors of this ancient mammal at Buffalo Crossing in Shelby County, a 1,000-acre ranch. You can also sample the meat prepared in a variety of ways at their restaurant.

Kentucky Culture

KENTUCKY BURGOO

Burgoo is a Kentucky favorite, slowly cooked outdoors in large black cast-iron kettles. Traditional burgoo was a stew consisting of whatever meat and vegetables pioneers could find, including rabbit, squirrel, and venison. Today's burgoo usually substitutes pork, beef, and chicken for the wild game. Anderson County holds a burgoo festival in September.

SLOW COOKER MOUNT ST. JOSEPH BURGOO

8 ounces cooked boneless skinless chicken, chopped
4 ounces cooked beef roast, chopped
1 cooked boneless pork chop, chopped
4 potatoes, cut into cubes
$\frac{1}{4}$ cup lima beans, cooked
$\frac{1}{4}$ cup navy beans, cooked
$3\frac{1}{4}$ cups chopped tomatoes
$1\frac{1}{2}$ cups shredded cabbage
$\frac{1}{4}$ cup whole kernel corn
$\frac{1}{3}$ cup Worcestershire sauce
2 tablespoons vinegar
1 teaspoon sugar
Salt and pepper to taste
3 cups water

Combine the chicken, beef, pork, potatoes, lima beans, navy beans, tomatoes, cabbage, corn, Worcestershire sauce, vinegar, sugar, salt, pepper and water in a slow cooker and mix well. Cook on Low for 8 hours. (You may substitute barbecued pork or mutton for one of the meats.) *Yield: 15 servings.*

DELECTABLE DAIRY DISHES
Cheese • Milk • Cream • Butter

DELECTABLE DAIRY DISHES
Cheese · Milk · Cream · Butter

4-H livestock projects are a long-standing tradition in Kentucky. From the club's beginning with rural youth to today, 4-H members raise animals and participate in shows and fairs. This future County Extension Agent shows her prize-winning Jersey heifer at a 1963 District Dairy Show in Somerset.

Dairy cows came to Kentucky with the early settlers and were often dubbed the "foster mothers of the human race." For generations, to have a cow of any of the six breeds was to be assured of a steady supply of nutritious fresh milk, cheese with high-quality protein, and butter for seasoning and baking.

As farming specialized and fewer families owned a cow, milk products were processed in local communities and delivered door to door. Refrigeration and transportation improved and products could be hauled longer distances, making it possible to process dairy products in fewer locations with distribution through grocery stores.

Many Kentucky dairy farms are located in the central part of the state, from the Ohio River to the Tennessee border. The average number of milk cows on Kentucky farms has declined steadily since 1986, but the average production per cow has increased. In 2001, producers sold 1.63 billion pounds of milk to plants and dealers, with 99 percent of the milk sold being fluid grade milk (used for drinking) and the remaining milk being manufacturing grade (used for making dairy products such as cheese). In that same year, sixteen Kentucky plants produced 14.7 million pounds of cottage cheese curd, 17.2 million pounds of creamed cottage cheese, and 9.5 million pounds of low-fat cottage cheese.

The value of milk produced during 2001 came to $269 million, but growth in supply outpaced growth in demand. Improved production and efficiency have kept milk prices low, while the cost of land, labor, and environmental regulations have caused some producers to close their dairy operations. Others have increased operations, with some returning to direct marketing of specialized, homestead-produced dairy products.

Spicy Two-Cheese Garden Appetizer

16 ounces fat-free cream cheese, softened
1 cup nonfat sour cream
2 tablespoons taco seasoning mix
1 cup mild or hot taco sauce
1 cup (4 ounces) shredded reduced-fat Cheddar cheese
$1/2$ cup chopped green onions
$1/2$ cup chopped green bell pepper
$1/2$ cup chopped tomato

Beat the cream cheese, sour cream and taco seasoning mix in a medium mixing bowl until smooth. Spread evenly on a 12- to 14-inch glass serving platter. Drizzle with the taco sauce. Sprinkle with the cheese, green onions, bell pepper and tomato. Chill, covered, until ready to serve. Serve with baked tortilla chips or snack crackers. *Yield: 10 servings.*

Campbellsville Cheese Ball

16 ounces cream cheese, softened
$2^1/2$ cups (10 ounces) shredded Cheddar cheese, at room temperature
1 tablespoon chopped pimento
1 tablespoon chopped onion
1 tablespoon chopped green bell pepper
2 teaspoons Worcestershire sauce
1 teaspoon lemon juice
1 cup finely chopped pecans

Combine the cream cheese and Cheddar cheese in a bowl and mix well. Add the pimento, onion, bell pepper, Worcestershire sauce and lemon juice and mix well. Chill, covered, in the refrigerator. Shape into 1 or 2 balls. Roll in the chopped pecans. *Yield: 32 servings.*

GLENDALE GOAT CHEESE WITH STRAWBERRY VINAIGRETTE

2/3 cup frozen strawberries
1/2 cup sugar
1/4 cup red wine vinegar
2 tablespoons minced red onion
1 tablespoon dry mustard
1/2 teaspoon salt
1/2 teaspoon lemon juice
1 cup olive oil
1 tablespoon poppy seeds
2 (5-ounce) logs soft fresh goat
    cheese

1 egg
1 tablespoon water
1/2 cup sliced almonds
1/2 cup flour
2 teaspoons butter, melted
Salt and pepper to taste
6 ounces mesclun or other salad
    greens

Process the strawberries, sugar, vinegar, onion, dry mustard, salt and lemon juice in a food processor until blended. Add the olive oil gradually, processing constantly. Add the poppy seeds. Process for 5 seconds.

Cut each log of goat cheese into 4 round slices. Pat each 1/2 inch thick. Whisk the egg and water in a small bowl until blended. Mix the almonds and flour in a bowl. Dip the cheese slices into the egg mixture and then into the almond mixture, pressing the almonds to adhere. Place the cheese slices in a glass baking dish. Drizzle lightly with the butter. Sprinkle with salt and pepper. Bake at 350 degrees for 10 minutes or until the almonds are light brown.

Divide the mesclun among 4 salad plates. Top each with 2 warm cheese slices. Drizzle with the strawberry vinaigrette and serve. *Yield: 4 servings.*

CARAWAY CHEESE CRISPS

1 1/2 cups flour
1/2 cup (1 stick) butter, softened
1 1/2 teaspoons caraway seeds
1/4 teaspoon salt
3 cups (12 ounces) shredded Cheddar cheese, at room temperature

Combine the flour, butter, caraway seeds, salt and cheese in a large bowl and mix well. Shape into 1/2-inch balls. Arrange 3 of the balls in a cluster on an ungreased baking sheet. Flatten with the bottom of a glass or your hand. Repeat with the remaining balls, placing each cluster 1/2 inch apart. Bake at 425 degrees for 10 to 12 minutes or until the clusters are crisp. Cool slightly before removing from the baking sheet. (These crisps are light and delicious.) *Yield: 30 servings.*

ICY TOMATO BUTTERMILK SOUP

1 (10-ounce) can tomato soup
2 medium tomatoes, diced
2 green onions, cut into 1-inch pieces
4 sprigs of fresh parsley
3/8 teaspoon red pepper sauce
2 cups cold buttermilk
1/4 cup chopped celery

Purée the canned soup, tomatoes, green onions, parsley and pepper sauce in a blender for 15 seconds. Add the buttermilk and process well. Pour into an airtight container. Stir in the celery. Chill, covered, for 3 to 4 hours to allow the flavors to blend. *Yield: 8 servings.*

Autumn Cheesy Soup

1/4 cup chopped onion
1 garlic clove, minced
3 tablespoons butter
1/4 cup flour
1/4 teaspoon pepper
2 cups milk

1 (14-ounce) can chicken broth
1/2 cup shredded carrots
1/4 cup chopped celery
2 cups (8 ounces) shredded Cheddar
   cheese or mozzarella cheese, or
   a combination of both

Sauté the onion and garlic in the butter in a large saucepan until the onion is transparent. Stir in the flour and pepper until smooth. Add the milk gradually, stirring constantly. Cook over medium heat until thickened and bubbly, stirring constantly.

Bring the broth, carrots and celery to a boil in a small saucepan. Simmer for 5 minutes or until the vegetables are tender. Add to the milk mixture and stir until blended. Stir in the cheese. Heat until the cheese is melted. Do not boil. Ladle into soup bowls. Garnish with chopped fresh or dried chives. *Yield: 4 servings.*

Taylor Cheesy Potato Soup

4 chicken bouillon cubes
5 cups water
1 cup sliced carrots
1 cup sliced celery
1 cup minced onion

6 medium potatoes, cut into cubes
2 (10-ounce) cans cream of chicken
   soup
12 to 16 ounces American cheese, cut
   into cubes

Dissolve the bouillon in the water in a large heavy stockpot. Add the carrots, celery, onion and potatoes. Cook until the vegetables are tender. Add the canned chicken soup and cheese. Reduce the heat to low. Simmer until the cheese melts. Ladle into soup bowls. Garnish with crumbled cooked bacon. (You may combine the first 6 ingredients in a slow cooker and cook on Low for 6 to 8 hours. Add the chicken soup and cheese 30 minutes before serving.) *Yield: 8 servings.*

Eggplant, Tomato and Goat Cheese Sandwiches

1¹/₂ cups chopped seeded tomatoes
¹/₄ cup chopped fresh basil
2 teaspoons red wine vinegar
Salt and pepper to taste
1 eggplant, cut lengthwise into slices
    ¹/₂ inch thick

2 tablespoons olive oil
6 large ¹/₂-inch-thick slices country-
    style French bread
9 ounces soft mild goat cheese

Combine the tomatoes, basil and vinegar in a small bowl and mix well. Season with salt and pepper.

Brush the eggplant slices lightly with some of the olive oil. Place on a grill rack. Grill over medium-high heat for 4 minutes on each side or until golden brown. Remove from the heat. Brush the bread lightly with the remaining olive oil. Place on a grill rack. Grill over medium-high heat for 2 minutes per side or until golden brown.

Arrange the bread on individual serving plates. Spread with the goat cheese. Top with the eggplant slices. Season with salt and pepper. Spoon the tomato mixture on top of each using a slotted spoon and spread to cover.
Yield: 6 servings.

Buttermilk Salad

1 (16-ounce) can pineapple
1 (6-ounce) package orange gelatin
2 cups buttermilk

8 ounces whipped topping, or 1 cup
    whipping cream, whipped

Bring the undrained pineapple to a boil in a saucepan. Add the gelatin. Cook until the gelatin is dissolved, stirring constantly. Remove from the heat to cool. Add the buttermilk. Fold in the whipped topping. Pour into a 9×13-inch glass dish. Chill until set. (You may substitute your favorite flavor of gelatin.)
Yield: 15 servings.

EIGHTY-EIGHT FOUR-CHEESE
EGGPLANT LASAGNA

1 cup low-fat ricotta cheese
1 cup low-fat cottage cheese
2 tablespoons parsley
1 teaspoon chopped garlic
1 (14-ounce) eggplant
5 cups spaghetti sauce
12 ounces lasagna noodles
4 ounces part-skim mozzarella cheese, grated
1/4 cup grated Parmesan cheese

Mix the ricotta cheese, cottage cheese, parsley and garlic in a bowl. Peel the eggplant and cut into slices 1/4 inch thick.

Pour 1 cup of the spaghetti sauce into a 9×13-inch baking dish sprayed with nonstick cooking spray. Arrange 1/3 of the noodles over the sauce so the noodles touch but do not overlap. Layer 1/2 of the eggplant over the noodles. Sprinkle with the mozzarella cheese. Spread 1 cup of the remaining sauce over the mozzarella cheese. Arrange 1/2 of the remaining noodles over the mozzarella cheese. Spread the ricotta cheese mixture over the noodles. Continue layering with the remaining eggplant, 1 cup of the remaining sauce, remaining noodles and the remaining sauce. Sprinkle with the Parmesan cheese.

Bake, tightly covered with foil, at 350 degrees for 1 hour. *Yield: 8 servings.*

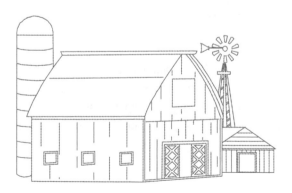

BLENDER CHEESE SOUFFLÉ

10 slices white bread, crusts trimmed
5 tablespoons butter
8 ounces sharp Cheddar cheese, cut into small cubes
4 eggs
2 cups milk
1 teaspoon salt
$^1/_4$ teaspoon cayenne pepper
$^1/_2$ teaspoon dry mustard

Spread the bread with the butter. Tear into small cubes. Process the bread cubes, cheese, eggs and milk $^1/_2$ at a time in a blender until thoroughly blended. Combine both batches in a large bowl. Stir in the salt, cayenne pepper and dry mustard. Pour into a greased 1$^1/_2$-quart baking dish. Bake at 350 degrees for 1 hour. Serve immediately. *Yield: 8 servings.*

COW DAYS COTTAGE CHEESE SOUFFLÉ

3 eggs, beaten
2 tablespoons flour
$^1/_2$ cup sugar
$^1/_2$ teaspoon lemon extract
1 pound small-curd cottage cheese
Cinnamon to taste

Combine the eggs, flour, sugar, lemon extract and cottage cheese in a large bowl and mix well. Pour into a nonstick 1-quart baking dish. Sprinkle with the cinnamon. Bake at 350 degrees for 30 minutes. *Yield: 8 servings.*

CELEBRATING OUR DAIRY INDUSTRY

Try your hand at milking a cow, win the milk mustache contest, or sample one of the prize-winning dairy recipes during local dairy celebrations and festivals across Kentucky. Kick off Dairy Month on the first Friday of June in Fleming County. On the third Friday and Saturday in September, take the family to Greensburg for Cow Days Festival. A calf is given away during the event, which also includes a hay bale tossing contest, milking a life-size fiberglass cow, arts and crafts, music and a quilt show.

CHEESE CASSEROLE

3 tablespoons butter
3 tablespoons flour
1 teaspoon salt
$^{1}/_{4}$ teaspoon pepper
3 cups milk, heated
10 round snack crackers
6 hard-cooked eggs, chopped
1 (2-ounce) jar pimento, drained
2 cups (8 ounces) shredded Cheddar cheese

Melt the butter in a 2-quart saucepan. Stir in the flour, salt and pepper. Add the milk gradually, stirring constantly. Cook until thickened, stirring constantly. Remove from the heat.

Crumble $^{1}/_{2}$ of the crackers into a 9×13-inch baking dish. Layer $^{1}/_{2}$ of the hard-cooked eggs, $^{1}/_{2}$ of the sauce, pimento, remaining hard-cooked eggs and remaining sauce in the prepared dish. Arrange the remaining crackers over the top. Sprinkle with the cheese. Bake at 325 degrees for 25 minutes.
Yield: 16 servings.

CHEESE RING

8 ounces sharp Cheddar cheese,
    shredded
1/2 cup crackers, crushed
1 (2-ounce) jar pimento, drained and
    chopped
1 cup milk

1/2 teaspoon celery seeds
1/4 teaspoon dry mustard
2 tablespoons vinegar
1/4 of the juice of 1 lemon
1 tablespoon sugar
2 eggs, beaten

Grease an 8-inch ring mold with butter or nonstick cooking spray. Mix the
cheese, crackers and pimento in a large bowl. Add the milk, celery seeds, dry
mustard, vinegar, lemon juice, sugar and eggs and mix well. Pour into the
prepared mold. Bake at 325 degrees for 1 hour. (You may fill the center of
the ring with peas, if desired.) *Yield: 10 servings.*

POPLAR PLAINS CHEESE PUDDING

5 slices bread
8 ounces extra-sharp Cheddar
    cheese, grated
3 eggs

2 cups skim or 2% milk
1 teaspoon salt
1 teaspoon dry mustard

Trim the bread. Cut each slice into 4 squares. Layer the cheese and bread
squares alternately in a buttered 1³/₄-quart baking dish, beginning and ending
with the cheese. Beat the eggs in a mixing bowl. Add the milk, salt and dry
mustard and blend well. Pour over the layers. Chill for 48 hours. Bake at
350 degrees for 45 minutes. *Yield: 6 servings.*

GRAVEL SWITCH TWIST CHEESE BREAD

1/2 cup milk
1 egg
3 tablespoons olive oil
1/4 cup water
1 teaspoon salt
2 teaspoons bread machine yeast
3 cups bread flour
1 cup (4 ounces) shredded sharp Cheddar cheese
1/2 cup (2 ounces) shredded Swiss cheese
1/4 cup grated Parmesan cheese
1 (15-ounce) can pizza sauce, heated
1 tablespoon grated Parmesan cheese

Add the milk, egg, olive oil, water, salt, yeast and bread flour to the bread machine pan in the order recommended by the manufacturer. Set the machine on the dough mode. When the cycle is complete, remove the dough to a floured surface. Knead in additional flour if needed to make the dough easy to handle.

Roll into a 12×18-inch rectangle. Sprinkle with a mixture of the Cheddar cheese, Swiss cheese and 1/4 cup Parmesan cheese to within 1/2 inch of the edges. Roll up tightly beginning at the long end and pinching the seam to seal. Place seam side down on a large greased baking sheet. Cut 1 inch deep lengthwise down the center to within 1/2 inch of the ends using a sharp knife. Shape into an "S" shape, keeping the cut side on top and tucking both ends under the center of the "S" to form a figure "8" and pinching the dough to join. Let rise, covered, in a warm draft-free place for 35 to 40 minutes or until doubled in bulk.

Bake at 350 degrees for 10 to 15 minutes. Cover with foil. Bake for 25 to 30 minutes longer or until golden brown. Remove from the baking sheet. Cut into slices and place on serving plates. Spoon the pizza sauce over the top and sprinkle with 1 tablespoon Parmesan cheese. *Yield: 16 servings.*

CHEDDAR CHEESE CASSEROLE BREAD

2 envelopes dry yeast
2 cups warm (105 to 115 degrees) milk
3 tablespoons sugar
1 tablespoon butter
$^1/_2$ teaspoon salt
$4^1/_2$ cups flour
6 ounces Cheddar cheese, cut into $^1/_2$-inch cubes

Dissolve the yeast in the warm milk in a large bowl. Add the sugar, butter and salt and stir until the butter is melted. Add 3 cups of the flour and stir until smooth. Stir in the remaining flour and cheese. Pour into a well-buttered 2-quart round baking dish. Cover with waxed paper. Let rise for 1 hour or until doubled in bulk. Remove the waxed paper. Bake at 350 degrees for 50 to 55 minutes or until golden brown. Remove from the oven and let cool for 10 minutes. Cut into 2-inch wedges and serve warm. *Yield: 15 servings.*

BAGDAD BREAKFAST CASSEROLE

1 pound sausage
3 cups milk
6 eggs
$^1/_2$ teaspoon dry mustard
$^1/_2$ teaspoon salt
6 slices bread, cut into cubes
8 ounces sharp Cheddar cheese, shredded

Crumble the sausage into a microwave-safe dish. Microwave on High for 7 minutes; drain. Process the milk, eggs, dry mustard and salt in a blender until blended. Spread the sausage and bread cubes in a 9×13-inch baking dish sprayed with nonstick cooking spray. Pour the egg mixture over the layers. Sprinkle with the cheese. Chill, covered, for 8 hours or longer. Bake at 350 degrees for 40 to 50 minutes or until set. Let stand for 5 minutes before serving. *Yield: 16 servings.*

Secret Family Recipe Banana Pudding

3 cups milk
3 eggs, beaten
1 cup sugar
2 tablespoons (heaping) self-rising
    flour

Salt to taste
1 (12-ounce) package vanilla wafers
3 or 4 bananas, sliced

Blend the milk and eggs in a double boiler. Add the sugar, flour and salt and mix well. Cook over medium heat for 15 minutes or until thickened, stirring constantly. Remove from the heat. Let stand for 1 hour, stirring occasionally.

Line the bottom of an 8×8-inch baking dish with a layer of vanilla wafers. Cover the vanilla wafers with a layer of bananas. Spread 1/3 of the pudding over the bananas. Arrange a layer of vanilla wafers on edge around the side of the dish. Repeat the layers of the remaining vanilla wafers, bananas and pudding twice. Chill, covered, in the refrigerator. *Yield: 8 servings.*

Southern Lassies

1/2 cup (1 stick) butter, softened
3 ounces cream cheese, softened
1 cup flour
1 cup chopped pecans

1 cup packed brown sugar
1 egg, beaten
1 tablespoon vanilla extract

Combine the butter, cream cheese and flour in a bowl and mix well using your hands. Shape into 24 small balls. Flatten into circles. Fit into miniature muffin cups, pressing to line up to the top edge. Fill each about 3/4 full of chopped pecans. Mix the brown sugar, egg and vanilla in a bowl. Spoon 1 tablespoon of the brown sugar mixture over the pecans into each cup. Bake at 350 degrees for 30 minutes or until light brown. *Yield: 24 servings.*

PULLED CREAM CANDY

3¹/₂ cups sugar	1 cup water
¹/₂ teaspoon salt	1 tablespoon butter
1 teaspoon vinegar	1 cup cream

Heat the sugar, salt, vinegar and water in a heavy saucepan until the sugar is melted. Stir in the butter. Add the cream gradually, stirring constantly. Cook to 252 degrees on a candy thermometer, hard-ball stage. Pour onto a cold marble slab. Do not scrape the bottom or side of the pan. Flip with a buttered spatula for 5 minutes or until cool enough to handle. Pull into long strands until the candy becomes opaque and elastic but still retains its satiny finish. Cut with buttered scissors. *Yield: 60 pieces.*

OLD-FASHIONED BROWN SUGAR ICING

¹/₂ cup (1 stick) butter	1 teaspoon vanilla extract
1 cup packed dark brown sugar	2¹/₄ cups confectioners' sugar
¹/₃ cup half-and-half	¹/₂ cup chopped pecans

Melt the butter in a heavy saucepan. Add the brown sugar. Bring to a boil over low heat, stirring constantly. Boil for 1 minute, stirring constantly. Remove from the heat. Add the half-and-half and mix well. Return to the heat and bring to a boil. Remove from the heat and cool slightly. Stir in the vanilla. Beat in the confectioners' sugar gradually until of a spreading consistency. Stir in the pecans. (The dark brown sugar gives this icing a distinctive flavor. It is best spread over a warm cake.) *Yield: 12 servings.*

Kentucky Culture

PULLED CREAM CANDY

Pulled cream candy has been an inexpensive tasty treat since the pioneer days. Traditionally, the candy was poured out onto an old meat platter before pulling. Modern candy makers use a chilled marble slab. They pull the candy until it lies flat on the marble and doesn't move or twitch when left alone. The candy is then cut into pieces with scissors. Making pulled candy can be quite an undertaking, but the end result will melt in your mouth and be well worth your aching arms.

An easier way to satisfy your sweet tooth is to visit one of the commercial producers in Garrard, Powell, and Montgomery Counties.

HOMEMADE ICE CREAM

Hand cranked ice cream was a treat to treasure on sunny days before air conditioning. Memories include wrapping blocks of ice in a towel and using the hammer to break them into chunks for the White Mountain oak barreled ice cream freezer. The smallest child always got the dubious honor of sitting on a blanket on top of the freezer to weigh it down during cranking. Children could hardly wait to let the ice cream ripen. A favorite version was creamy vanilla ice cream with chunks of homegrown peaches, eaten on the front porch.

VANILLA ICE CREAM

$1/4$ cup flour
2 cups sugar
$1/2$ teaspoon salt
3 eggs, lightly beaten

4 cups milk, scalded
1 cup heavy cream
1 (14-ounce) can evaporated milk
2 tablespoons vanilla extract

Mix the flour, sugar and salt in a double boiler. Add the eggs and mix well. Add the scalded milk gradually, stirring constantly. Cook for 10 minutes, stirring constantly. Remove from the heat to cool. Stir in the cream, evaporated milk and vanilla. Pour into a 4- to 6-quart ice cream freezer container. Freeze using the manufacturer's directions. *Yield: 16 ($1/2$-cup) servings.*

BUTTERMILK PIE

$1/2$ cup (1 stick) butter, softened
$1 1/2$ cups sugar
3 tablespoons flour
3 eggs, beaten
1 cup buttermilk

1 teaspoon lemon juice
1 teaspoon vanilla extract
$1/8$ teaspoon salt
1 unbaked (9-inch) pie shell
Grated nutmeg to taste

Beat the butter and sugar in a large mixing bowl until light and fluffy. Add the flour, eggs, buttermilk, lemon juice, vanilla and salt and mix well. Pour into the pie shell. Sprinkle lightly with nutmeg. Bake at 350 degrees for 1 hour or until the top is golden brown. *Yield: 8 servings.*

BUTTERSCOTCH PIE

1¹/₂ cups packed brown sugar
¹/₄ cup cornstarch
3 tablespoons flour
2 cups milk
3 egg yolks, beaten
2 tablespoons margarine
1 teaspoon vanilla extract
1 baked (9-inch) pie shell
Meringue (below)

Mix the brown sugar, cornstarch and flour in a double boiler. Add just enough milk gradually to form a paste. Add the egg yolks and the remaining milk and mix well. Cook over hot water until thickened, stirring constantly. Remove from the heat. Stir in the margarine and vanilla. Pour into the pie shell. Spread the meringue over the top, sealing to the edge. Bake at 350 degrees for 13 minutes or until the meringue is golden brown. *Yield: 8 servings.*

MERINGUE

3 egg whites
1 teaspoon vanilla extract
¹/₂ teaspoon cream of tartar
¹/₂ cup sugar

Beat the egg whites, vanilla and cream of tartar in a mixing bowl until soft peaks form. Add the sugar 1 tablespoon at a time and beat until stiff peaks form. *Yield: 8 servings.*

MILK IN YOUR DAILY DIET

How much calcium do you need? Ages one through ten and over the age of twenty-five need 800 milligrams daily. Ages eleven through twenty four and pregnant or nursing women need 1,200 milligrams a day. Low-fat milk products provide the calcium you need without the fat and calories.

Compare 8-ounce servings: whole milk has 150 calories, 8 grams of fat, and 291 milligrams of calcium; 2 percent milk has 120 calories, 5 grams of fat, and 297 milligrams of calcium; 1 percent milk has 102 calories, 3 grams of fat, and 300 milligrams of calcium; skim milk has 86 calories, 0 fat, and 302 milligrams of calcium. If your calcium is low, you have a higher risk for osteoporosis, colon cancer, high blood pressure, and kidney stones.

CHESS PIE

1/2 cup (1 stick) butter, softened
1 1/2 cups sugar
1 tablespoon cornmeal
2 tablespoons flour
2 eggs
Juice of 1/2 lemon
1 teaspoon vanilla extract
1/2 cup milk
1 unbaked (9-inch) pie shell

Beat the butter, sugar, cornmeal and flour in a mixing bowl. Add the eggs, lemon juice, vanilla and milk and mix well. Pour into the pie shell. Bake at 425 degrees for 10 minutes. Reduce the oven temperature to 325 degrees. Bake for 30 to 35 minutes longer. *Yield: 8 servings.*

BANDANA PEACH PIE

1/2 cup (1 stick) butter
1 cup flour
1/2 cup pecans, finely chopped
8 ounces cream cheese, softened
1 cup confectioners' sugar
1 cup whipped cream
1 (21-ounce) can peach pie filling

Cut the butter into the flour in a bowl until crumbly. Stir in the pecans. Press into an 8-inch deep-dish pie plate. Bake at 350 degrees for 15 minutes. Remove from the oven to cool. Beat the cream cheese and confectioners' sugar in a mixing bowl until smooth and creamy. Add the whipped cream and mix well. Pour into the cooled piecrust. Chill for 2 hours. Spread the peach pie filling over the top of the pie. Chill until ready to serve. *Yield: 8 servings.*

BOUNTIFUL BEANS AND GRAINS
Soybeans · Corn · Wheat

Sponsor: Kentucky Soybean Association and Promotion Board

Bountiful Beans and Grains
Soybeans · Corn · Wheat

Learning by doing applies to youth and adults alike. Cooperative Extension Agents often teach through demonstrations and hands-on experiences, today as well as in years past, as shown in this mid-twentieth-century bread making activity. Safe food preparation and nutrition are major programs of the Cooperative Extension Service.

Soybeans have been used as food for over 2,000 years. The Chinese discovered and later cultivated wild soybeans. Early missionaries brought news of soybeans and soyfoods to Europe from China as long ago as 1665. Soybeans came to the United States as ballast on trading ships in the 1800s. The U.S. soyfoods industry began in the early 1900s when Asian-American companies introduced tofu and soymilk and developed the meat alternative products for ethnic, vegetarian, and "health food" markets.

In the 1950s, new technologies were developed to improve flavor and texture of soy proteins and soyfoods. In the 1970s and 1980s, hundreds of entrepreneur soyfood companies were established, and tofu and tempeh were introduced to non-Asian consumers as a meat alternative. In the 1900s, the introduction of Americanized products such as frozen entrées, veggie burgers, tofu hot dogs, and flavored and fortified soymilks increased consumer appeal. The millennium brought in a tidal wave of soy products as the soyfoods market attracted the food industry's major players and supermarkets became major outlets for soyfoods. The endorsements of health benefits brought further growth, with hundreds of new varieties of products entering the marketplace.

Historically, the soyfoods industry has outpaced the overall food industry. The Kentucky Soybean Association and Promotion Board has been instrumental in the growth of the soyfoods and soy products markets. Formed in 1970, they support research and promotion of soy products for uses such as biodiesel fuel, candles, lotions, and carpet backing. Promotional materials and projects such as the Soyfoods Recipe Contest and Ag Education in the Classroom help educate consumers about soy products and their uses. Soy is no longer just a niche market. Soyfoods can be found in grocery stores all over Kentucky, and sales are projected to hit $4.4 billion by 2004.

Apple Broccoli Soy Salad

2 cups chopped unpeeled Gala apples
2 cups broccoli florets
¹/₂ cup golden raisins
2 ribs celery, chopped
1 cup seedless grape halves
Garlic Mustard Vinaigrette (below)
1 cup edamame (green soybeans), cooked and shelled
¹/₄ cup cashews, roasted

Combine the apples, broccoli, raisins, celery and grapes in a large salad bowl and toss to mix. Chill, covered, until ready to serve.

To serve, pour Garlic Mustard Vinaigrette over the salad and toss to coat. Sprinkle with the edamame and cashews. *Yield: 15 servings.*

Garlic Mustard Vinaigrette

1 garlic clove, minced
1 tablespoon chopped red onion
¹/₃ cup red wine vinegar
¹/₄ cup sugar, or an equivalent amount of sugar substitute
¹/₂ teaspoon salt
1 teaspoon prepared mustard
1 tablespoon celery seeds
1 cup vegetable oil

Process the garlic, onion, vinegar, sugar, salt, mustard and celery seeds in a blender until smooth. Add the oil 1 tablespoon at a time, processing constantly. Chill, covered, until ready to serve. *Yield: 15 servings.*

Types of Tofu

Firm tofu is dense and solid and holds up very well in stir-fry dishes, soups, or on the grill—anywhere that you want the tofu to maintain its shape. Firm tofu is also higher in protein, fat, and calcium than other forms of tofu.

Soft tofu is a good choice for recipes that call for blended tofu or in Oriental soups.

Silken tofu is a creamy, custard-like product which works well in puréed or blended dishes.

EDAMAME

Edamame, pronounced ed-a-mom-ay, is from the Japanese word for green soybeans. You can find edamame in the pod or shelled at grocery or specialty food stores, farmers' markets, and roadside stands. Frozen vegetable mixtures of broccoli, carrots, and green edamame beans are also available. In fresh beans, look for bright green pods without signs of yellowing.

HAIL CAESAR SALAD

3 chicken breasts
1/4 cup Italian salad dressing
3 cups edamame pods (green soybeans)
1/4 cup water
1/2 teaspoon minced garlic

1 head romaine, torn into pieces
2 teaspoons lemon juice
3 tablespoons olive oil
3/4 cup bottled fat-free Caesar salad dressing
1 cup croutons

Place the chicken in a sealable plastic bag. Pour the Italian salad dressing over the chicken and seal the bag. Marinate in the refrigerator for 15 minutes. Drain the chicken, discarding the marinade. Place on a grill rack. Grill until a meat thermometer inserted into the thickest portion registers 170 degrees. Cut the chicken into strips, discarding the skin and bones.

Place the edamame pods and the water in a microwave-safe container. Microwave, covered, on High for 5 to 7 minutes. Shell the edamame, discarding the pods. (You should have 1 cup edamame.)

Rub the garlic on the inside of the salad bowl. Add the romaine. Add the lemon juice, olive oil and Caesar salad dressing and toss to coat. Add the chicken and edamame. Top with the croutons. *Yield: 6 servings.*

GREEN SOYBEANS AND CORN

1 (16-ounce) package edamame (green soybeans)
1 (10-ounce) package frozen white Shoe Peg corn

1/3 cup water
1 teaspoon cilantro
1 tablespoon butter

Cook the edamame using the package directions; drain. Shell the edamame, discarding the pods. Combine with the corn in a medium saucepan and mix well. Add the water, cilantro and butter. Bring to a boil and reduce the heat. Simmer for 4 to 6 minutes or until tender. *Yield: 8 servings.*

Vegi-Sausage Corn Bread

10 vegi-sausage links
1 (8-ounce) package corn bread mix
½ cup (2 ounces) shredded sharp
   Cheddar cheese
3 medium green onions with tops,
   chopped (about ¼ cup)

Place the sausage in a microwave-safe dish. Microwave on High for 2 minutes.

Prepare the corn bread using the package directions, adding the cheese and green onions. Pour into an 8-inch cast-iron skillet sprayed with nonstick cooking spray. Arrange the sausage in spoke-fashion on top. Bake at 400 degrees for 20 minutes or until the corn bread is golden brown. Cut into wedges. Serve with salsa and nonfat sour cream. *Yield: 8 servings.*

Benton Tofu Banana Bread

8 ounces (1 cup) tofu
2 ripe bananas, cut into quarters
½ cup soybean oil
½ cup honey
1 cup all-purpose flour
1½ teaspoons baking soda
1 teaspoon cinnamon
1 cup whole wheat flour
½ cup chopped walnuts

Purée the tofu, bananas, oil and honey in a blender, scraping down the side with a rubber scraper. Sift the all-purpose flour, baking soda and cinnamon into a medium bowl. Stir in the whole wheat flour and walnuts using a fork. Stir in the banana mixture. Spoon into a greased and floured 5×9-inch loaf pan, spreading to make the top level. Bake at 350 degrees for 1 hour or until a wooden pick inserted into the center comes out clean. Cool in the pan on a wire rack for 10 minutes. Loosen around the edges with a knife. Invert onto the rack and cool completely. *Yield: 12 servings.*

Tips for Using Textured Soy Protein

Use textured soy protein to replace all or part of the ground meat in almost any recipe. Replace ¼ of the ground beef in meat loaf and burgers.

Generally, textured soy protein will triple in volume when hydrated. For example, 1 pound dry textured soy protein will make about 3 pounds hydrated textured soy protein.

For 1 pound of ground beef, substitute 1½ cups dry textured soy protein and hydrate with 1½ cups water.

Fiesta Roll-Ups

1 (15-ounce) can whole kernel corn
    or Mexicorn, drained
1 cup edamame (green soybeans),
    cooked and shelled
5 ounces textured soy protein (TSP),
    cooked

2 cups (8 ounces) shredded
    Monterey Jack cheese
2 cups mild thick salsa
8 flour tortillas

Combine the corn, edamame, textured soy protein, cheese and $1/2$ cup of the salsa in a bowl and mix well. Spoon evenly over each tortilla and roll up to enclose the filling. Place seam side down in a microwave-safe dish. Top with the remaining salsa. Microwave on High for 5 to 7 minutes or until heated through. *Yield: 8 servings.*

This is the 2001 Soy Food Recipe Champion, Debbie Troop from Owensboro, Kentucky.

Tofu Enchiladas

2 (10-ounce) packages silken firm
    tofu, drained
$3/4$ cup (3 ounces) shredded
    Monterey Jack cheese
3 tablespoons chopped cilantro
3 tablespoons minced onion

$1/2$ teaspoon chili powder
1 (15-ounce) can low-sodium
    enchilada sauce
6 (6-inch) corn tortillas
2 tablespoons chopped green onions
2 tablespoons sliced black olives

Combine the tofu, cheese, cilantro, onion and chili powder in a medium bowl and mix well. Heat the enchilada sauce in a small saucepan. Dip each tortilla quickly into the heated sauce and place on a flat surface. Top with about $1/3$ cup of the tofu mixture and roll up tightly. Place seam side up in an 8×8-inch shallow baking dish. Pour the remaining enchilada sauce over the top. Bake at 350 degrees for 20 to 25 minutes or until heated through. Sprinkle with the green onions and black olives. *Yield: 6 servings.*

Soy Food Lasagna Delight

2 (14-ounce) cans diced tomatoes
1 (15-ounce) can tomato sauce
1 cup chopped fresh mushrooms
1/2 cup chopped green bell
    pepper
1 teaspoon chopped garlic
1/2 teaspoon oregano
1 cup frozen soy burger
1 cup frozen soy sausage

1 (10-ounce) package frozen
    chopped spinach, thawed and
    drained
16 ounces ricotta cheese
1 medium onion, chopped
8 ounces lasagna noodles, cooked
    and drained
16 ounces mozzarella cheese,
    shredded

Combine the tomatoes, tomato sauce, mushrooms, bell pepper, garlic, oregano, soy burger and soy sausage in a large skillet and mix well. Cook over low heat for 10 minutes.

Mix the spinach, ricotta cheese and onion in a medium bowl. Alternate layers of the noodles, spinach mixture and tomato soy mixture in a 9×13-inch baking dish until all ingredients are used. Top with the mozzarella cheese. Bake at 325 degrees for 45 minutes or until bubbly and the cheese is golden brown. *Yield: 6 servings.*

This is the 2000 Soy Food Recipe Champion, Katrina Randolph from Princeton, Kentucky.

SUSAN'S TOFU STIR-FRY

1 package angel hair pasta nest
1 cup water
1 cup textured soy protein (TSP) chunks
1 tablespoon ketchup
2 cups hot water
1 cup frozen Soya-Wise
2 tablespoons soybean oil
1 (16-ounce) package fresh or frozen broccoli stir-fry
1 cup fresh mushrooms, or 1 (6-ounce) can low-sodium sliced mushrooms, drained (optional)
1/2 orange bell pepper, cut into strips
1/2 yellow bell pepper, cut into strips
1/2 red bell pepper, cut into strips
1 cup shelled edamame (green soybeans)
2 tablespoons chopped onion
1/2 cup whole sugar snap peas
1/2 cup hot water
1 tablespoon cornstarch
1/3 cup Splenda
1/4 cup low-sodium soy sauce
1 tablespoon spicy brown mustard
3/4 cup cold water
1/2 cup soynuts, chopped

Bring 2 inches of water in a Dutch oven to a boil. Add the pasta nest. Cook for 2 minutes; drain. Place on a large serving plate and keep warm.

Combine 1 cup water, TSP chunks and ketchup in a microwave-safe bowl. Let stand for 10 minutes. Microwave on High for 10 minutes.

Combine 2 cups hot water and the Soya-Wise in a bowl. Let stand for 10 minutes to soak up the liquid; drain.

Heat the soybean oil in a wok to 350 degrees. Add the TSP mixture, Soya-Wise, broccoli stir-fry, mushrooms, bell peppers, edamame, onion and sugar snap peas. Cook for 5 minutes, adding the remaining 1/2 cup hot water as needed.

Mix the cornstarch, Splenda, soy sauce, mustard and 3/4 cup cold water in a bowl. Add to the wok and stir quickly. Spoon over the pasta nests. Sprinkle with the soynuts. (Textured soy protein (TSP) or textured vegetable protein (TVP) and Soya-Wise can be found in all natural food stores and many grocery stores.)*Yield: 6 servings.*

This is the 2002 Soy Food Recipe Champion, Susan Sexton from Franklin, Kentucky.

Dreamy Strawberry Tofu

1¹/₂ cups tofu
1¹/₂ cups fresh strawberries
¹/₂ cup sugar
¹/₄ cup soybean oil

1 tablespoon lemon juice
1 teaspoon vanilla extract
¹/₈ teaspoon salt

Process the tofu, strawberries, sugar, soybean oil, lemon juice, vanilla and salt in a food processor or blender until smooth and creamy. Pour into individual serving dishes. Chill for 8 to 12 hours. Garnish with fresh strawberries before serving. (You may also use as a pie filling and pour into a baked pie shell.)
Yield: 7 servings.

This homemaker from the 1930s proudly shows her trellis of ten toe gourds. Gardens were a staple for Kentucky families throughout the twentieth century. Today families without a backyard garden can enjoy farm fresh produce at their local Farmers' Market.

"R" FARM (CORN MAZE)

If you're looking for an a"maze"ing experience, travel to picturesque Maysville during the fall and wander through the two-acre corn maze at "R" Farm on Strodes Run Road. Schedule your visit during the "Corn Maze Under the Stars" weekend so you can experience a hayride and marshmallow roast around a campfire. The farm's annual "Pumpkinfest" features a plentiful patch of pumpkins as well as a kid's rodeo, petting zoo, greased pig contest, cloggers, a talent contest, horse-drawn wagon rides, crafts, collectibles, and food booths. In addition, "R" Farm offers group and school tours during the harvest season.

CHERRY TOFU DELIGHT

8 ounces low-fat cream cheese,
   softened
1 (10-ounce) package firm tofu
8 ounces lite whipped topping

3 tablespoons honey
1/4 teaspoon almond extract
1 (21-ounce) can lite cherry
   pie filling

Process the cream cheese and tofu in a blender until smooth. Fold in the whipped topping, honey and almond extract. Stir in the pie filling. Spoon into a serving dish. Chill until set. Garnish with crushed crunchy cereal. *Yield: 14 servings.*

CHOCOLATE TOFU SWIRL CHEESECAKE

1 (9-ounce) package chocolate
   wafers
1/4 cup sliced almonds
6 tablespoons soy margarine, melted
16 ounces lite cream cheese
1 (10 1/2-ounce) package silken tofu
1 1/4 cups sugar

4 eggs
3 tablespoons lemon juice
2 cups lite sour cream
1/3 cup sugar
1 teaspoon vanilla extract
2 tablespoons chilled chocolate syrup

Process the wafers in a food processor or blender until chopped. Add the almonds and margarine and process until finely ground. Spread evenly and press onto the bottom and up the side of a 10-inch springform pan.

Process the cream cheese, tofu and 1 1/4 cups sugar in a food processor or blender until smooth. Add the eggs and lemon juice and process until smooth. Pour into the prepared pan. Bake at 350 degrees for 50 minutes. Remove from the oven. Reduce the oven temperature to 300 degrees.

Combine the sour cream, 1/3 cup sugar and vanilla in a bowl and mix well. Spread over the cheesecake. Drizzle the chocolate syrup over the top and swirl gently with a knife to marbleize. Bake for 20 to 25 minutes. Remove from the oven. Let stand for 1 hour. Chill, covered, for 8 to 12 hours. Serve plain or top with fresh fruit. *Yield: 10 servings.*

PUMPKIN TOFU PIE

1 unbaked (9-inch) pie shell
1 cup soft tofu
1¹/₂ cups cooked pumpkin
¹/₂ cup sugar
2 tablespoons cornstarch

¹/₂ cup milk
1 egg (optional)
2 or 3 teaspoons pumpkin pie spice
¹/₂ teaspoon salt (optional)

Bake the pie shell at 400 degrees for 5 to 7 minutes. Remove from the oven to cool. Reduce the oven temperature to 350 degrees.

Process the tofu, pumpkin, sugar, cornstarch, milk, egg, pumpkin pie spice and salt in a blender or food processor until smooth. Pour into the cooled pie shell. Cover the edges with foil. Bake for 1 hour or until a knife inserted in the center comes out almost clean. Cool on a wire rack. Serve at room temperature. Store in the refrigerator. *Yield: 8 servings.*

BROCCOLI CORN BREAD

1 small onion, chopped
¹/₂ cup (1 stick) margarine, melted
4 eggs
1 (8¹/₂-ounce) package corn
    muffin mix
¹/₂ cup small curd cottage cheese

1 (10-ounce) package frozen
    chopped broccoli, cooked and
    drained
¹/₂ cup (2 ounces) shredded Cheddar
    cheese or Swiss cheese

Sauté the onion in the margarine in a skillet. Beat the eggs in a mixing bowl until light and fluffy. Add the corn muffin mix and cottage cheese and mix well. Stir in the sautéed onion, broccoli and Cheddar cheese. Pour into a greased 9×13-inch baking dish. Bake at 375 degrees for 25 to 30 minutes or until golden brown. Cut into 2-inch squares. (This is a delicious accompaniment to burgoo or soups. This recipe also freezes well.) *Yield: 20 servings.*

CAYCE CORN BREAD

2 eggs
1 cup sour cream
1 cup cream-style corn
$^1/_2$ cup vegetable oil
1 cup self-rising cornmeal
$^1/_3$ cup chopped mild peppers
$^1/_2$ cup (2 ounces) shredded Cheddar cheese

Combine the eggs, sour cream, corn, oil and cornmeal in a bowl and mix well. Pour into a 9×9-inch baking pan sprayed with nonstick cooking spray. Layer the peppers over the top. Sprinkle with the cheese. Bake at 400 degrees for 20 to 25 minutes or until golden brown. *Yield: 9 servings.*

TRADITIONAL HOT WATER CORN BREAD

2 cups sifted stone-ground cornmeal
$^1/_2$ teaspoon salt
1 tablespoon sugar
$^3/_4$ cup powdered milk
Boiling water
Vegetable oil for deep-frying

Mix the cornmeal, salt, sugar and powdered milk in a large bowl. Add enough boiling water to make a ball, stirring constantly. Roll a small amount of the mixture at a time into an oblong shape. (This shape will cook better and faster.) Drop into hot oil in a deep fryer. Deep-fry until light brown or your favorite color of doneness. (There are a lot of ways to make corn bread. This is an old country favorite.) *Yield: 8 servings.*

Old-Fashioned Stone-Ground Corn Bread

1¹/₂ cups yellow-stone ground cornmeal
1 cup flour
¹/₂ teaspoon salt
1 tablespoon baking powder
¹/₄ teaspoon baking soda
1 egg, lightly beaten
1¹/₂ teaspoons vegetable oil or melted butter
1¹/₂ cups buttermilk

Mix the cornmeal, flour, salt, baking powder and baking soda in a medium bowl. Add the egg, oil and buttermilk and mix well. Pour into a hot greased 8-inch cast-iron skillet. Bake at 425 degrees until golden brown. *Yield: 8 servings.*

Light and Tasty Corn Cakes

2 eggs, beaten
2 cups milk
¹/₄ cup canola oil
1¹/₃ cups cornmeal
¹/₂ teaspoon salt

Combine the eggs, milk and canola oil in a bowl and mix well. Mix the cornmeal and salt together. Stir into the egg mixture. Drop 2 tablespoons of the batter at a time into a hot greased skillet or onto a hot greased griddle. (Be sure and stir the batter well each time, as the cornmeal will settle.) Cook until the tops are covered with bubbles and turn. Cook until golden brown. Serve with hot butter. *Yield: 24 servings.*

Kentucky Culture

Corn Bread

Corn in the form of cornmeal is the main ingredient for corn bread. Corn bread was being made by Native Americans long before the first Europeans settled the colonies. Pioneers often referred to corn bread as "pone," a term adapted from the Algonquin language. "Pone" was a simple mixture of cornmeal, salt, and water.

From colonial times to the present, corn bread has remained a staple in the diet of most Kentuckians. Corn bread recipes differ from region to region. Northern corn breads use significant amounts of sugar and flour, while Southern corn breads use little, if any, sugar or flour.

Cumberland Cornmeal Muffins

2 tablespoons vegetable oil
1 cup fresh ground cornmeal
1 cup self-rising cornmeal
1/4 teaspoon baking soda

1/4 teaspoon salt
1 egg
1 tablespoon vegetable oil
1 1/4 cups buttermilk

Spoon 1/2 teaspoon of oil into each muffin cup. Heat in a 450-degree oven until hot. Mix the fresh ground cornmeal, self-rising cornmeal, baking soda and salt in a bowl. Add the egg, 1 tablespoon oil and buttermilk and mix well. Pour into the prepared muffin cups. Bake for 15 to 20 minutes or until golden brown. *Yield: 12 servings.*

Kentucky Spoon Bread

4 cups milk
1 cup white cornmeal
1 1/2 teaspoons salt

3 tablespoons butter or margarine
4 eggs, beaten

Heat the milk in a double boiler over boiling water until tiny bubbles appear around the edges. Add the cornmeal gradually, whisking constantly. Add the salt and butter. Cook for 10 to 12 minutes or until the butter melts and the mixture is thickened, stirring constantly. Remove from the heat. Add about 1/4 of the hot mixture gradually to the beaten eggs; add the egg mixture to the remaining hot mixture, stirring constantly. Spoon into a lightly greased 2-quart baking dish or soufflé dish. Bake at 425 degrees for 40 to 45 minutes or until golden brown. Serve with butter. *Yield: 10 servings.*

The origin of spoon bread is unclear. Although its ingredients vary in recipes across the South, it's usually based on cornmeal and baked like a casserole. Its pudding-like texture makes it soft enough to eat with a spoon. Serve with most any type of meat.

Old Time Turkey Corn Bread Dressing

4 cups corn bread crumbs
4 cups crumbled light bread or
    biscuits
1 cup chopped onion
4 eggs

2 tablespoons poultry seasoning
Salt and pepper to taste
Sage to taste
2 cups (about) turkey broth
2 tablespoons margarine, sliced

Mix the corn bread crumbs, light bread crumbs, onion, eggs, poultry seasoning, salt, pepper and sage in a large bowl. Add enough of the turkey broth to moisten. Spoon into a buttered 7×11-inch glass baking dish. Place thin slices of the margarine over the top. Bake at 350 degrees for 35 minutes or until light brown. *Yield: 12 servings.*

Boone Corn Bread Salad

2 (6-ounce) packages sweet yellow
    corn bread mix
1 cup sour cream
1 cup mayonnaise
1 envelope ranch salad dressing mix
2 (16-ounce) cans light kidney beans,
    rinsed and drained
2 (11-ounce) cans sweet niblet corn,
    drained

1 medium bell pepper, chopped
2 large tomatoes, chopped
10 slices bacon, cooked and
    crumbled
2 cups (8 ounces) shredded Mexican
    cheese
12 green onions, chopped

Prepare and bake the corn bread mix using the package directions. Let stand until cool. Crumble the corn bread.

    Mix the sour cream, mayonnaise and ranch salad dressing mix in a bowl. Layer the corn bread, kidney beans, corn, bell pepper, tomatoes and bacon $1/2$ at a time in a large serving bowl. Pour the sour cream mixture over the layers. Sprinkle with the cheese and green onions. Garnish with additional chopped tomatoes. *Yield: 16 servings.*

Caramel Candy Corn

8 quarts popped popcorn
2 cups dry roasted peanuts
1 cup (1 stick) margarine
$^1/_2$ cup light corn syrup
1 cup sugar

1 cup packed brown sugar
1 teaspoon salt
1 teaspoon baking soda
1 teaspoon vanilla extract
1 teaspoon butter flavoring

Mix the popcorn and peanuts in a 9×17-inch foil baking pan. Bring the margarine, corn syrup, sugar, brown sugar and salt to a boil in a large saucepan and reduce the heat. Simmer for 5 minutes, stirring occasionally. Remove from the heat. Stir in the baking soda, vanilla and butter flavoring quickly. Pour over the popcorn mixture and stir to mix well. Bake at 250 degrees for 1 hour, stirring every 15 minutes. Remove from the oven and stir occasionally while the popcorn mixture cools. Store in an airtight container. *Yield: 22 (1$^1/_2$-cup) servings.*

Microwave Caramel Corn

1 cup packed brown sugar
$^1/_2$ cup (1 stick) margarine
$^1/_4$ cup corn syrup

$^1/_2$ teaspoon salt
$^1/_2$ teaspoon baking soda
4 quarts popped popcorn

Bring the brown sugar, margarine, corn syrup and salt to a boil in a microwave-safe container. Microwave on High for 2 minutes. Stir in the baking soda. Place the popcorn in a large microwave-safe container. Pour the brown sugar mixture over the popcorn and toss to coat. Microwave on High for 1$^1/_2$ minutes; stir. Microwave for 1$^1/_2$ minutes longer; stir. Pour into a shallow pan to cool.
Yield: 16 (1$^1/_2$-cup) servings.

Shiloh Sweet Popcorn

1 cup popcorn, popped
¹/₂ cup (1 stick) butter
¹/₄ cup honey
1 cup packed brown sugar

Spread the popped popcorn in a large oblong baking pan. Bring the butter, honey and brown sugar to a boil in a saucepan. Boil for 5 minutes. Pour over the popcorn and toss to coat. Bake at 250 degrees for 1 hour, stirring every 15 minutes. (Mixture must be stirred every 15 minutes.) Remove from the oven to cool. Break into pieces. *Yield: 10 servings.*

Butler Beer Bread

3 cups self-rising flour
3 tablespoons sugar
1 (12-ounce) can beer

Combine the self-rising flour, sugar and beer in a bowl and mix well. Pour into a greased 5×9-inch loaf pan. Bake at 325 degrees for 55 minutes. (You may substitute 3 cups all-purpose flour, 4¹/₂ teaspoons baking powder and ³/₄ teaspoon salt for the self-rising flour.) *Yield: 12 servings.*

Kentucky Culture

Popcorn in Kentucky

According to legend, Iroquois Indians provided a deerskin bag of popped corn to the colonists as a gift at the first Thanksgiving feast at Plymouth Rock. As settlers moved west, they brought seed with them. Popcorn also has a long history in Kentucky, as well as being a healthful snack. In the 1930s popcorn was introduced into Calloway County, which grew to be the one-time "popcorn capital of the world." Over 20,000 acres of popcorn was grown and processed in six companies in the county. Today there is one remaining processing plant in the county and several others in the state.

HORSE CAVE DILLY BREAD

2 envelopes dry yeast
$^1/_2$ cup lukewarm water
2 cups cream-style cottage cheese
2 tablespoons butter
$^1/_4$ cup sugar
2 tablespoons dried onion flakes
4 teaspoons dillseeds
4 teaspoons salt
1$^1/_2$ teaspoons baking soda
2 eggs, beaten
5 cups flour

Dissolve the yeast in the lukewarm water in a small bowl. Heat the cottage cheese in a saucepan until lukewarm. Add the butter and remove from the heat.

Combine the cottage cheese mixture, sugar, onion flakes, dillseeds, salt, baking soda and eggs in a large bowl and mix well. Stir in the yeast mixture. Add the flour gradually, stirring to form a soft dough. Grease the top and cover. Let rise until doubled in bulk. Punch the dough down. Divide the dough into 2 equal portions. Shape each portion into a loaf. Place in two greased 5×9-inch loaf pans. Grease the top of the loaves and cover. Let rise until doubled in bulk. Bake at 350 degrees for 30 to 40 minutes or until golden brown. *Yield: 20 servings.*

GOLD MEDAL GARDENS

Vegetables · Fruit

EGGS
SQUASH
CABBAGE
TOMATOES
CUCUMBERS
POTATOES
GREEN BEANS
SWEET CORN
PEACHES

FARM FRESH
PRODUCE

Sponsor: West Kentucky Corporation

GOLD MEDAL GARDENS
Vegetables · Fruit

Through the decades, Kentucky families grew large gardens and preserved the bounty for the winter months. Homemakers canned and dried fruits and vegetables long before grocery stores and supermarkets were the norm. Although the size of gardens and the amount of home-preserved food has decreased, canning and freezing fruits and vegetables continues to be popular among modern families. The Cooperative Extension Service provides guidelines, directions, and recipes for safe home food preservation.

As Kentucky producers have diversified their farm enterprises, there has been significant growth in fruit and vegetable production. Vegetable production has doubled in the past five years. Current estimates indicate 12,000 acres of vegetables are being produced with a value of 28 to 32 million dollars annually. About half of the acreage is marketed through direct sales and half through wholesale. Vegetable marketing has expanded through the efforts of four marketing co-operatives: Green River Produce in Hart County, West Kentucky Growers in Daviess County, Cumberland Farm Products in Wayne County, and Central Kentucky Vegetable Growers in Scott County. Vegetable production is centered around each of the co-ops, with West Kentucky leading the way with over 800 acres of sweet corn and a large acreage of tomatoes near Paducah.

Fruit production has remained more stable, with an estimated 5,000 acres of fruit and nut production valued at $8 million annually. Tree fruit has not significantly expanded since 1997. A decrease in apple production has been offset by an increase in peach production. Berries and grapes are currently the fastest growing sectors of any produce groups in Kentucky. Berry production has increased to around 400 acres. Grape acreage is going to increase significantly as the wine industry is developed. Increased income from the expanded berry and grape crops will be slight due to the young plantings.

Health, taste, and convenience are important to today's consumers. They want nutrient-dense, safe, high-quality foods. Ready-to-eat, prepackaged foods like salad greens make it easier to prepare healthy meals in a short period of time. The popularity of ethnic foods with tomatoes or specialty greens has also increased demand for fresh vegetables. As producers target the consumers' needs, the opportunities for expanding vegetable and fruit production will continue to increase.

MAYS LICK CREAM OF ASPARAGUS SOUP

1/2 cup chopped onion
1 tablespoon vegetable oil
2 (14-ounce) cans chicken broth
2 1/2 pounds fresh asparagus, trimmed and cut into 1-inch pieces
1/4 teaspoon tarragon
1/4 cup (1/2 stick) butter or margarine
1/4 cup flour
1/2 teaspoon salt
1/4 teaspoon white pepper
3 cups half-and-half
1 1/2 teaspoons lemon juice

Sauté the onion in the oil in a large saucepan over medium heat until tender. Add the broth, asparagus and tarragon. Simmer for 8 to 10 minutes or until the asparagus is tender. Purée the asparagus mixture 1/3 at a time in a blender or food processor.

Melt the butter in a Dutch oven or stockpot. Stir in the flour, salt and white pepper. Cook for 2 minutes or until golden brown, stirring constantly. Add the half-and-half gradually, stirring constantly. Stir in the puréed asparagus mixture and lemon juice. Cook until heated through. *Yield: 8 (1-cup) servings.*

Mays Lick, Kentucky, hosts an annual Asparagus Festival each May. In an effort to market agriculture, a banker in the early 1900s declared Mays Lick the "asparagus bed of Mason County," in reference to its fertile soil. Along with fun and fellowship, the festival features asparagus specialties: breads, soups, crepes, pies, hors d'oeuvre, and even pickled asparagus.

Kentucky Culture

LEATHER BRITCHES

"Leather britches" is the name given to snap beans that are dried whole in the pod by stringing with a needle and thread and hanging to dry. Once dried, the beans are packed loosely in a storage container and stored in a cool, dry place or refrigerator. The term "leather britches" originated from the Cherokee Indians because the beans' dried, shriveled appearance resembled leather britches. Shuck beans, shucky beans, or fodder beans are leather britches without the pod. They are shelled before cooking.

BLUEGRASS ASPARAGUS QUICHE

1 refrigerator pie pastry	3 eggs
8 ounces asparagus	1 cup half-and-half
2 green onions, sliced	$1/2$ teaspoon salt
1 tablespoon flour	$1/4$ teaspoon basil
8 ounces Swiss cheese, shredded	$1/8$ teaspoon pepper

Line a 9-inch quiche dish with the pie pastry, trimming the edge. Prick the pastry lightly with a fork. Bake at 425 degrees for 7 minutes or until the crust is set but not brown. Remove from the oven. Reduce the oven temperature to 350 degrees.

Trim the asparagus spears, discarding the tough ends. Heat $1/2$ inch of water in a 10-inch skillet over high heat. Add the asparagus. Cook, covered, for 3 minutes; drain and cool. Reserve 3 asparagus spears for the top. Cut the remaining spears into 1-inch pieces.

Combine the asparagus pieces, green onions and flour in a medium bowl and toss to mix well. Layer the asparagus mixture and cheese in the prebaked crust. Beat the eggs, half-and-half, salt, basil and pepper in a bowl until smooth. Pour over the layers. Bake for 25 minutes. Remove from the oven. Cut the reserved asparagus spears into halves lengthwise. Arrange cut side down on top of the quiche. Bake for 5 to 10 minutes longer or until a knife inserted in the center comes out clean. Let stand for 10 minutes before serving. *Yield: 6 servings.*

LEATHER BRITCHES

2 cups dried snap beans in the pods	4 slices fresh bacon, or $1/2$ cup jowl bacon, or 1 teaspoon bouillon
6 cups water	granules

Place the beans in a 5-quart saucepan and cover with water. Bring to a boil and reduce the heat. Simmer for 1 hour. Remove from the heat and drain. Rinse the beans thoroughly twice. Return to the saucepan. Add 6 cups water and bacon. Cook, covered, for 5 to 6 hours or until tender. (If you choose to use the jowl bacon, soak in cold water to cover for 1 hour to reduce the excess salt.) *Yield: 6 servings.*

Sweet-and-Sour Green Beans

4 cups (1 quart) green beans
4 slices bacon
2 medium onions, sliced
1 tablespoon dry mustard

1 teaspoon salt
2 tablespoons brown sugar
2 tablespoons sugar
1/4 cup vinegar

Cook the green beans in water to cover in a saucepan until tender. Drain, reserving 1 cup of the liquid. Fry the bacon in a skillet until crisp. Remove the bacon to paper towels to drain. Drain the skillet. Add the onions to the skillet. Sauté until brown and transparent. Stir in the dry mustard, salt, brown sugar and sugar. Add the reserved liquid and vinegar. Bring to a boil. Add the green beans and bacon. Simmer, covered, for 15 minutes. Serve with a slotted spoon.
Yield: 8 servings.

Harvard Beets

1/3 cup sugar
1/2 teaspoon salt
1 tablespoon cornstarch
1/2 cup water

1/2 cup vinegar
2 tablespoons butter or margarine
1 teaspoon minced onion (optional)
3 cups hot diced cooked beets

Combine the sugar, salt, cornstarch and water in a double boiler and mix well. Stir in the vinegar. Cook over boiling water until thickened and smooth, stirring constantly. Add the butter, onion and beets. Cook for 20 minutes.
Yield: 6 servings.

This recipe was from a foods lesson for Homemaker Clubs in 1952. Greens were cooked and pressed in a ring mold, then inverted onto a serving platter, and beets were used to fill the center of the ring of greens.

Kentucky Culture

Picking Wild Greens

In past years, farm families would walk their hillsides in last year's corn patch in early April looking for wild greens such as Shepherd's Sprout, Wild Lettuce, Lambs' Quarter, Shoney, Poke, Hog Mustard, Wild Cabbage, Dandelion, or Narrow Dock. When enough greens had been gathered for a mess, the family would return to the house, wash the greens, place them in a pot with a piece of bacon and cook until they were done. The broth the greens were cooked in was called "potlikker," and with crumbled-up corn bread, this was a tasty treat for dinner!

Big Creek Broccoli Salad

1 bunch broccoli, cut into bite-size pieces
1 bunch seedless red grapes, cut into halves (about 1½ cups)
1 medium red onion, sliced
1 (24-ounce) bottle sweet Vidalia onion salad dressing, ranch salad dressing,
    Catalina salad dressing, or sweet-and-sour salad dressing
2 medium red apples, chopped
½ cup peanuts
½ cup bacon bits

Combine the broccoli, grapes and onion in a bowl and toss to mix. Add the
salad dressing and toss to coat. Marinate, covered, in the refrigerator until
ready to serve. Add the apples, peanuts and bacon bits and toss to mix. (Try
using a different one of the salad dressings for a different taste each time.)
Yield: 10 servings.

Broccoli Raisin Salad

1 bunch broccoli, cut into bite-size pieces
1 cup golden raisins
1 medium onion, sliced
⅔ cup sugar
2 tablespoons vinegar
¾ cup mayonnaise-type salad dressing
10 slices bacon, cooked and crumbled

Combine the broccoli, raisins and onion in a bowl and toss to mix. Mix the
sugar, vinegar and mayonnaise-type salad dressing in a bowl. Pour over the
broccoli mixture and toss to coat. Marinate, covered, in the refrigerator for
8 to 12 hours. Stir in the bacon just before serving. (For variety, try adding
nuts, dried cranberries, orange slices, celery, mandarin oranges, strawberries,
grapes or water chestnuts.) *Yield: 8 servings.*

BROCCOLI PLATTER

2 pounds fresh broccoli, or 2 (10-
    ounce) packages frozen broccoli
Salt to taste
2 tablespoons minced onion
2 tablespoons butter
1 cup sour cream

$^1/_2$ teaspoon poppy seeds
$^1/_2$ teaspoon paprika
$^1/_4$ teaspoon salt
$^1/_8$ teaspoon cayenne pepper
$^1/_3$ cup chopped salted cashews

Trim the broccoli and cut into spears. Cook the broccoli in a small amount of water in a 3-quart saucepan for 12 to 15 minutes or until tender-crisp; drain. Season with salt to taste.

Sauté the onion in the butter in a skillet. Remove from the heat. Combine the sautéed onion mixture, sour cream, poppy seeds, paprika, $^1/_4$ teaspoon salt and cayenne pepper in a double boiler. Cook over boiling water until heated through, stirring frequently.

Arrange the broccoli spears on a heated platter. Pour the warm sauce over the top. Sprinkle with the chopped cashews. *Yield: 8 servings.*

SCALLOPED CABBAGE

4 cups shredded cabbage
1 teaspoon salt
$^1/_4$ teaspoon pepper
2 tablespoons flour
$^1/_3$ cup shredded Cheddar cheese
3 tablespoons butter

1 teaspoon salt
$^1/_4$ teaspoon pepper
1 tablespoon sugar
$^1/_2$ cup bread crumbs
1 cup hot milk

Drop the cabbage into boiling water in a large saucepan. Boil for 15 minutes; drain. Layer $^1/_2$ of the cabbage in a large buttered baking dish. Season with 1 teaspoon salt and $^1/_4$ teaspoon pepper. Sprinkle with the flour and cheese. Dot with $^1/_2$ of the butter. Top with the remaining cabbage. Season with 1 teaspoon salt and $^1/_4$ teaspoon pepper. Sprinkle with the sugar. Dot with the remaining butter. Sprinkle with the bread crumbs. Pour the hot milk over the layers. Bake at 400 degrees for 20 to 30 minutes or until the crumbs are golden brown. *Yield: 10 servings.*

SPICED RED CABBAGE

$1/2$ medium head red cabbage, chopped
1 tablespoon vegetable oil
$1/2$ cup chopped onion
2 medium tart apples, cut into quarters
3 tablespoons tarragon vinegar or red wine vinegar

1 tablespoon sugar
1 bay leaf
1 teaspoon salt, or to taste
$1/4$ teaspoon pepper
$1/8$ teaspoon ground cloves

Boil the cabbage in water to cover in a large stockpot for 1 minute. Drain and return the cabbage to the stockpot. Add the oil, onion, apples, vinegar, sugar, bay leaf, salt, pepper and cloves and stir to mix well. Simmer, covered, until the cabbage is tender. Discard the bay leaf before serving. *Yield: 6 servings.*

MOREHEAD MARINATED CARROTS

2 pounds carrots, sliced
1 cup tomato soup
1 bell pepper, chopped
1 onion, chopped
1 tablespoon Worcestershire sauce

$3/4$ cup vinegar
1 tablespoon dry mustard
$1/4$ cup vegetable oil
1 cup sugar
Salt and pepper to taste

Cook the carrots in a small amount of water in a saucepan until tender; drain. Spoon the carrots into a large bowl.

Combine the soup, bell pepper, onion, Worcestershire sauce, vinegar, dry mustard, oil, sugar, salt and pepper in a saucepan and mix well. Bring to a boil. Boil for 2 to 3 minutes. Pour over the carrots. Marinate, covered, in the refrigerator until ready to serve. Serve cold using a slotted spoon. *Yield: 6 servings.*

CARROT PINEAPPLE CAKE WITH WALNUT CREAM CHEESE FROSTING

2 cups flour
2 teaspoons baking soda
1 teaspoon salt
1 teaspoon cinnamon
2 cups grated carrots
2 cups sugar

1 1/2 cups vegetable oil
4 eggs
1 (8-ounce) can crushed pineapple
Walnut Cream Cheese Frosting
    (below)

Line three 9-inch cake pans with waxed paper. Grease and flour the prepared pans. Sift the flour, baking soda, salt and cinnamon together. Beat the carrots, sugar and oil in a mixing bowl. Add the eggs 1 at a time, beating well after each addition. Add the flour mixture and mix well. Fold in the undrained pineapple. Pour into the prepared cake pans.

Bake at 350 degrees for 35 to 40 minutes, adjusting the pans as needed for even baking. Cool slightly in the pans. Invert onto wire racks. Peel the waxed paper gently from the layers. Let stand until cool. Spread Walnut Cream Cheese Frosting between the layers and over the top and side of the cake. (To make lining the cake pans a snap, invert one of the cake pans over 3 layers of waxed paper. Use the pan as a template to cut all 3 liners at once. This cake is moist and freezes well.) *Yield: 24 servings.*

WALNUT CREAM CHEESE FROSTING

8 ounces cream cheese, softened
1/2 cup (1 stick) butter, softened
4 cups confectioners' sugar

1 teaspoon vanilla extract
1 cup chopped English walnuts

Beat the cream cheese and butter in a mixing bowl until creamy. Add the confectioners' sugar gradually, beating constantly and scraping the side of the bowl frequently. Add the vanilla and beat until smooth. Fold in the walnuts. *Yield: 24 servings.*

Beaumont Inn's Corn Pudding

Recipe courtesy of Charles M. Dedman, Chef,
Beaumont Inn, Harrodsburg

2 cups white whole kernel corn, or fresh corn from the cob	1 teaspoon salt
¹⁄₂ cup flour	¹⁄₄ cup (¹⁄₂ stick) butter, melted
4 teaspoons (heaping) sugar	4 eggs
	4 cups (1 quart) milk

Combine the corn, flour, sugar, salt and butter in a bowl and stir to mix well.
Beat the eggs and milk in a mixing bowl. Stir into the corn mixture. Pour into
a baking dish. Bake at 450 degrees for 40 to 45 minutes or until set, stirring
vigorously with a long-prong fork 3 times every 10 minutes, disturbing the top
as little as possible. *Yield: 8 servings.*

Cadiz Cucumber Salad

2 green bell peppers, thinly sliced	3 cups sugar
3 or 4 cucumbers, thinly sliced	¹⁄₄ cup salt
4 or 5 onions, thinly sliced	1 tablespoon celery seeds
2 cups white vinegar	

Combine the bell peppers, cucumbers and onions in a 1-gallon container with a
tight-fitting lid. Combine the vinegar, sugar, salt and celery seeds in a bowl and
stir until the sugar is dissolved. Pour over the vegetables. Marinate, covered, in
the refrigerator for 3 to 4 days before serving. (You may use 1 green and 1 red
bell pepper.) *Yield: 12 servings.*

Almond Bibb Salad

1 head Bibb lettuce or romaine, torn
1/4 head iceberg lettuce, torn
1/2 cup thinly sliced celery
2 green onions, thinly sliced
1/4 cup soybean oil
2 tablespoons sugar, or an equivalent
    amount of sugar substitute
2 tablespoons wine vinegar
1 tablespoon snipped fresh parsley
1/2 teaspoon salt
1/8 teaspoon red pepper sauce
1 (11-ounce) can mandarin oranges,
    drained
1/2 cup sliced almonds, toasted
1 purple onion, sliced (optional)

Place the Bibb lettuce, iceberg lettuce, celery and green onions in a large sealable plastic bag and seal the bag. Store in the refrigerator until ready to serve.

Mix the soybean oil, sugar, wine vinegar, parsley, salt and red pepper sauce in a jar with a tight-fitting lid. Chill, covered, until ready to serve.

To serve, pour the dressing over the lettuce mixture and seal the bag. Shake the bag well to coat. Arrange the lettuce mixture on individual salad plates. Top with the mandarin oranges, almonds and purple onion rings. *Yield: 6 servings.*

Bibb lettuce was developed by Major John Bibb in the backyard of his home, "Grey Gables" (Bibb-Burnley House), Frankfort. He moved to Frankfort in 1856 and shared his seeds and plants with friends. Soon it became known as Bibb lettuce and became commercially produced in 1935.

Kentucky Culture

SHIITAKE MUSHROOMS

Shiitake mushrooms are produced on logs from some of Kentucky's best forest trees, including white ash, white oak, yellow poplar, sugar maple, and sweet gum. Mushroom spores are injected into the logs, and the logs rest for one year while the spores produce roots. At the end of the year, the logs are soaked, and in the spring, mushrooms begin to form. Mushrooms are harvested by cutting them away from the log and are an excellent crop for farmers wanting to diversify their operations. Estill County hosts the Mountain Mushroom Festival each spring.

WOLFE WILTED LETTUCE

4 cups leaf lettuce, torn into pieces
1 small onion, chopped, or 4 green
   onions, chopped
4 radishes, thinly sliced
6 slices bacon

2 tablespoons vinegar
1 teaspoon brown sugar
1/4 teaspoon dry mustard
1/4 teaspoon salt
1/8 teaspoon pepper

Toss the lettuce, onion and radishes in a large salad bowl. Cook the bacon in a skillet until crisp. Remove the bacon to paper towels to drain, reserving the drippings in the skillet. Add the vinegar, brown sugar, dry mustard, salt and pepper to the drippings in the skillet. Bring to a boil, stirring constantly. Pour over the lettuce mixture and toss to coat. Crumble the bacon and sprinkle over the top. Serve immediately. *Yield: 4 servings.*

STUFFED MUSHROOMS

2 tablespoons butter
1 medium Vidalia onion, finely
   chopped
1/2 cup chopped pepperoni
1/4 cup finely chopped green, red and
   yellow bell peppers
1 garlic clove, minced
3/4 cup crushed butter crackers
   (about 12 crackers)

3 tablespoons grated Parmesan
   cheese
1/2 cup (2 ounces) shredded
   mozzarella cheese
1 tablespoon snipped fresh parsley
1/2 teaspoon tarragon
1/4 teaspoon oregano
1/3 cup chicken broth
12 to 15 shiitake mushroom caps

Melt the butter in a large skillet. Add the onion, pepperoni, bell peppers and garlic. Sauté until tender but not brown. Add the cracker crumbs, Parmesan cheese, mozzarella cheese, parsley, tarragon and oregano and mix well. Stir in the chicken broth. Spoon into the mushroom caps. Place in a shallow baking pan. Pour about 1/4 inch of water in the bottom of the pan. Bake at 325 degrees for 20 to 25 minutes. Serve warm. (You may assemble the mushrooms the night before and chill in the refrigerator. Place in the baking pan and add the water just before baking.) *Yield: 12 servings.*

144

Estill Shiitake Soup

7 1/2 cups hot water
1 tablespoon chicken bouillon
    granules
4 ounces carrots, cut into 1/4-inch
    slices
4 ounces shiitake mushroom caps,
    cut into 1/4-inch slices

2 cups snow peas, trimmed and cut
    lengthwise into halves
1/4 cup thinly sliced green onions
1/4 teaspoon white pepper

Combine the water, bouillon, carrots and shiitake mushrooms in a saucepan. Simmer over low heat for 10 minutes or until the carrots are almost tender. Add the snow peas, green onions and white pepper. Bring to a boil. Boil for 2 minutes or until the snow peas are tender. Serve immediately. *Yield: 4 servings.*

Rigatoni with Shiitake Mushrooms and Kielbasa

6 ounces rigatoni or other large
    tubular pasta
Salt to taste
1/4 cup vegetable oil
1/2 small onion, chopped

4 garlic cloves, finely chopped
1 ounce shiitake mushrooms, thinly
    sliced
4 ounces kielbasa, julienned

Cook the pasta in boiling salted water to cover in a large saucepan for 10 minutes or until al dente; drain.

Heat the oil in a skillet over medium heat. Add the onion and garlic. Sauté for 1 minute. Add the shiitake mushrooms and kielbasa. Sauté for 2 minutes. Season with salt. Spoon over the pasta and toss to coat. Serve immediately. (You may add 3/4 cup heavy cream to the shiitake mushroom mixture and cook over low heat until the cream thickens. Continue to cook for 5 minutes or until thickened, stirring constantly and adding some milk if the mixture is too thick. This sauce is also good reheated.) *Yield: 4 servings.*

Pickled Dilled Okra

7 pounds small okra pods
2 garlic cloves, cut into quarters
$2/3$ cup canning or pickling salt
6 small hot peppers
4 teaspoons dillseeds
6 cups water
6 cups vinegar

Rinse and trim the okra. Fill 8 sterilized 1-pint jars firmly with the whole okra pods, leaving $1/2$ inch headspace. Place $1/4$ of a garlic clove in each jar. Bring the salt, hot peppers, dillseeds, water and vinegar to a boil in a large saucepan. Pour over the okra, leaving $1/2$ inch headspace; seal with 2-piece lids. Process in a boiling water bath for 15 minutes. *Yield: 64 servings.*

Bowling Green Pepper Casserole

3 or 4 green bell peppers, cut into large pieces
Salt to taste
38 saltine crackers (1 sleeve), crushed
3 cups (12 ounces) shredded Cheddar cheese
$1/4$ cup ($1/2$ stick) margarine
1 cup (about) milk

Boil the large bell pepper pieces in salted water to cover in a saucepan until tender; drain. Layer the crackers, cheese, bell pepper pieces and margarine $1/2$ at a time in a greased $1^{1}/_{2}$-quart baking dish. Pour the milk over the layers to almost cover. Bake at 350 degrees for 30 minutes or until slightly set. *Yield: 6 servings.*

BAKED POTATO SOUP

12 slices bacon
2/3 cup margarine
2/3 cup flour
1 cup milk
4 large potatoes, baked, peeled and
 cubed

4 green onions, chopped
1 1/4 cups (5 ounces) shredded
 Cheddar cheese
1 cup sour cream
1 teaspoon salt
1 teaspoon pepper

Cook the bacon in a skillet until crisp; drain. Crumble the bacon. Melt the margarine in a stockpot or Dutch oven over medium heat. Whisk in the flour until smooth. Stir in the milk gradually. Cook until thickened, whisking constantly. Stir in the potatoes and green onions. Bring to a boil and reduce the heat, stirring frequently. Simmer for 10 minutes. Stir in the bacon, cheese, sour cream, salt and pepper. Cook until the cheese is melted, stirring frequently. (This is a great way to use leftover baked potatoes.) *Yield: 6 servings.*

PARTY POTATO SALAD

6 cups chopped cooked potatoes
3 hard-cooked eggs, chopped
1/4 cup chopped pimentos
1 medium bell pepper, chopped
3/4 cup chopped onion
3/4 cup sweet pickle relish
Salt to taste

1/2 cup vinegar
1/2 cup sugar
1 tablespoon flour
1 teaspoon salt
1 egg, beaten
1 cup mayonnaise-type salad dressing

Combine the potatoes, hard-cooked eggs, pimentos, bell pepper, onion, pickle relish and salt to taste in a large bowl and toss to mix well. Mix the vinegar, sugar, flour, 1 teaspoon salt and egg in a microwave-safe bowl. Microwave on Low for 1 minute. Whisk until blended. Microwave for 1 minute. Whisk until blended. Continue to microwave at 30-second intervals until thickened, whisking after each interval. Let stand until cool. Add the salad dressing and mix well. Pour over the potato mixture and toss to coat well. Spoon into a serving dish. Garnish with paprika and parsley. Chill until ready to serve. *Yield: 12 servings.*

Spicy Red Potato Salad

15 red potatoes
5 medium hard-cooked eggs,
    chopped
1 cup chopped onion
1/2 cup chopped celery
1/2 cup chopped green bell pepper

1 1/2 cups mayonnaise
2 teaspoons garlic powder
1/2 teaspoon salt
1/2 teaspoon black pepper
1/4 teaspoon red pepper flakes

Scrub the potatoes. Place in a saucepan and cover with water. Cook over medium-high heat for 20 minutes or until soft. Drain and rinse under cold water. Drain again and blot with paper towels until room temperature. Place the potatoes in a bowl and chop coarsely with a knife. Add the hard-cooked eggs, onion, celery, bell pepper and mayonnaise and mix well. Stir in the garlic powder, salt, black pepper and red pepper flakes. Chill, covered, for 1 hour before serving. *Yield: 12 servings.*

Roasted Potato Salad

2 1/2 pounds new potatoes
3 tablespoons olive oil
1 garlic clove, minced
1/8 teaspoon salt
1/8 teaspoon pepper

1 1/2 tablespoons red wine vinegar
1 tablespoon Dijon mustard
2 tablespoons olive oil
2 teaspoons chopped chives

Scrub the potatoes. Cut the potatoes into 1 1/2-inch pieces. Combine the potatoes, 3 tablespoons olive oil and garlic in a bowl and toss to coat. Place in a single layer in a 7×11-inch baking dish. Season with the salt and pepper. Bake at 400 degrees for 30 minutes or until brown on all sides, turning once or twice.

Beat the red wine vinegar and Dijon mustard in a small bowl. Add 2 tablespoons olive oil and beat well. Combine with the potatoes in a bowl and toss to mix well. Sprinkle with the chives. *Yield: 6 servings.*

CRUSTY GARLIC AND ROSEMARY POTATOES

2 pounds small red potatoes,
    scrubbed and cut into quarters
3 large garlic cloves, thinly sliced
    lengthwise

1 tablespoon olive oil
$^1/_2$ to 1 teaspoon rosemary, crumbled
Salt and pepper to taste

Steam the potatoes, covered, in a steamer over boiling water for 8 to 10 minutes or until fork tender. Sauté the garlic in the olive oil in a nonstick skillet over medium heat until pale golden brown. Add the potatoes, rosemary, salt and pepper. Sauté over medium-high heat for 5 minutes or until the potatoes are golden brown. *Yield: 4 servings.*

One benefit from the long hours of growing a garden and preserving its results is to be able to exhibit the best jars at the county fair and perhaps win a ribbon and prize money. Competition was often stiff (and still is!) at many local fairs, such as this one in 1934 in Harlan County. Winning a blue ribbon for canned fruits and vegetables or fresh garden produce continues to be an honor.

Pulaski Pumpkin Corn Soup

3 cups fresh corn from the cob
1½ cups water
2 garlic cloves, minced
¾ teaspoon salt
½ teaspoon white pepper
3 cups chicken broth

3 cups mashed cooked pumpkin
¼ cup fresh lime juice
1 tablespoon grated gingerroot
1½ teaspoons grated lime zest
½ cup whipping cream

Combine the corn and water in a saucepan. Cook, covered, over medium heat for 10 minutes or until tender. Process in a food processor for 2 minutes or until smooth. Pour through a wire-mesh strainer into a bowl, discarding the pulp. Combine the corn mixture, garlic, salt, white pepper and chicken broth in a Dutch oven. Bring to a boil over medium heat. Reduce the heat to low. Stir in the pumpkin. Simmer for 10 minutes, adding additional chicken broth if needed.

Cook the lime juice and ginger in a small saucepan over medium heat for 2 minutes. Remove from the heat. Pour through a wire-mesh strainer into a small mixing bowl, discarding the pulp. Add the lime zest and whipping cream. Beat at medium speed until soft peaks form. Ladle the soup into individual serving bowls and dollop with the ginger-lime cream. *Yield: 8 servings.*

Pumpkin Bread

3 cups flour
3 cups sugar
1½ teaspoons salt
1 teaspoon cinnamon
½ teaspoon allspice
½ teaspoon baking powder
2 teaspoons baking soda

4 eggs
2 cups pumpkin
⅔ cup water
⅔ cup vegetable oil
1 teaspoon vanilla extract
1 cup chopped walnuts

Mix the flour, sugar, salt, cinnamon, allspice, baking powder and baking soda together. Beat the eggs, pumpkin, water, oil and vanilla in a mixing bowl until smooth. Add the flour mixture and walnuts and mix well. Spoon into 3 greased 5×8-inch loaf pans. Bake at 350 degrees for 1 hour or until the loaves test done. *Yield: 36 servings.*

TOASTED PUMPKIN SEEDS

2 cups fresh pumpkin seeds
1¹/₂ tablespoons vegetable oil

Salt to taste

Rinse and wipe the pulp from the fresh pumpkin seeds, being sure to remove all pulp. Coat the pumpkin seeds with the oil. Spread in a thin layer on a baking sheet. Bake at 350 degrees for 20 to 30 minutes or until the seeds "pop," watching carefully to prevent burning. Sprinkle with salt. Store in an airtight container. (Clean out those Halloween pumpkins for a crunchy snack.) *Yield: 16 servings.*

RHUBARB PIE

1¹/₂ cups sugar
3 tablespoons flour
¹/₂ teaspoon nutmeg
1 tablespoon butter

2 eggs, well beaten
3 cups uncooked cut-up rhubarb
2 refrigerator pie pastries

Beat the sugar, flour, nutmeg and butter in a mixing bowl until blended. Add the eggs and mix well. Stir in the rhubarb. Line a 9-inch deep-dish pie plate with 1 of the pie pastries. Pour in the rhubarb mixture. Top with the remaining pie pastry, trimming and fluting the edge and cutting vents.

Bake at 450 degrees for 10 minutes. Reduce the oven temperature to 350 degrees. Bake for 30 minutes longer. (To prevent the edge from overbrowning, cut a piece of foil 2 inches wide and place around the outside edge while baking.) *Yield: 8 servings.*

Although often thought of as a fruit, rhubarb is actually a vegetable. The edible stem is cooked and used for desserts, sauces, side dishes, and preserves. The leaves of the rhubarb are toxic.

Strawberry Spinach Salad

1 pound spinach, trimmed
1 pint strawberries, cut into slices
1/2 cup sugar
2 tablespoons sesame seeds
1 tablespoon poppy seeds
1 1/2 teaspoons minced onion

1/4 teaspoon Worcestershire sauce
1/4 teaspoon paprika
1/4 cup cider vinegar
1/2 cup corn oil or soy bean oil
1/4 cup almonds

Rinse the spinach and pat dry. Toss the spinach and strawberries in a large salad bowl. Process the sugar, sesame seeds, poppy seeds, onion, Worcestershire sauce, paprika and vinegar in a blender. Add the corn oil gradually, processing constantly. Pour over the spinach mixture and toss to coat. Sprinkle with the almonds. Serve immediately. *Yield: 8 servings.*

Spinach Salad

1 pound spinach, trimmed
1 (15-ounce) package fresh bean
    sprouts, or 1 (14-ounce) can
    bean sprouts, drained
1 (8-ounce) can sliced water
    chestnuts, drained

6 slices bacon, cooked and crumbled
3 hard-cooked eggs, sliced
3/4 cup sugar
1/3 cup vinegar
1 tablespoon Worcestershire sauce
1 cup vegetable oil

Rinse the spinach and pat dry. Tear into bite-size pieces and place in a salad bowl. Add the bean sprouts, water chestnuts, bacon and hard-cooked eggs and toss to mix. Process the sugar, vinegar and Worcestershire sauce in a blender. Add the oil gradually, processing constantly. Pour over the spinach mixture and toss to coat. *Yield: 8 servings.*

Butternut Squash Bread

3½ cups flour
2 teaspoons baking soda
½ teaspoon baking powder
1½ teaspoons salt
1 teaspoon ground cloves
1 teaspoon cinnamon
⅔ cup shortening

2⅔ cups sugar
4 eggs
2 cups mashed cooked butternut
squash
⅓ cup water
⅔ cup chopped pecans
⅔ cup chopped dates

Sift the flour, baking soda, baking powder, salt, cloves and cinnamon together. Cream the shortening and sugar in a mixing bowl until light and fluffy. Add the eggs 1 at a time, beating well after each addition. Add the squash and water and mix well. Beat in the flour mixture gradually. Stir in the pecans and dates. Pour into 2 nonstick 5×9-inch loaf pans. Bake at 350 degrees for 1 hour. (You may substitute pumpkin or cushaw for the butternut squash.) *Yield: 24 servings.*

Baked Summer Squash

3 pounds yellow summer squash,
cooked and drained
½ cup chopped onion
2 eggs
1 tablespoon sugar

1 teaspoon salt, or to taste
1 teaspoon pepper
1 cup bread crumbs or cracker
crumbs
½ cup (1 stick) butter, melted

Mash the squash in a bowl. Add the onion, eggs, sugar, salt, pepper, half the bread crumbs and half the butter and mix well. Spoon into a 2-quart baking dish. Pour the remaining butter over the top. Sprinkle with the remaining bread crumbs. Bake, uncovered, at 375 degrees for 1 hour. *Yield: 8 servings.*

GRANDMA'S CUSHAW PIE

2 cups cooked cushaw
1 (14-ounce) can sweetened
  condensed milk
2 eggs
1 teaspoon cinnamon

$^1/_2$ teaspoon ginger
$^1/_2$ teaspoon nutmeg
$^1/_2$ teaspoon salt
1 unbaked (9-inch) pie shell

Combine the cushaw, condensed milk, eggs, cinnamon, ginger, nutmeg and salt in a bowl and mix well. Pour into the pie shell. Bake at 425 degrees for 15 minutes. Reduce the oven temperature to 350 degrees. Bake for 35 to 40 minutes longer or until a knife inserted 1 inch from the edge of the pie comes out clean. Remove to a wire rack to cool. *Yield: 8 servings.*

Kentucky gardens often feature a large green-and-white-striped crookneck squash—the cushaw. Planted along with corn, this winter squash is gathered after the first frost and stored in a cool, dry place. Families prefer cushaw over its cousin, the pumpkin, because of the hard shell and "keeping" ability. Cushaw can be prepared and substituted for other winter squash varieties, such as pumpkin, butternut, and Hubbard. Look for cushaw during the fall at roadside stands and farmers' markets.

SWEET POTATOES STUFFED WITH APPLES

4 medium sweet potatoes
3 cups chopped peeled apples
$^1/_4$ cup ($^1/_2$ stick) margarine, melted

$^1/_2$ cup sugar
1 teaspoon cinnamon

Rinse the sweet potatoes and pat dry. Place on the oven rack. Bake at 425 degrees for 30 minutes. Cool for a few minutes. Cut the sweet potatoes into halves. Scoop the sweet potato pulp from each half into a bowl, reserving the shells. Reduce the oven temperature to 300 degrees. Sauté the apples in the margarine in a skillet until tender. Add the sweet potato pulp, sugar and cinnamon and mix well. Spoon into the reserved shells. Place in a 9×13-inch baking dish. Bake until heated through. *Yield: 4 servings.*

Sweet Potato Casserole

Kentucky Fresh

Recipe courtesy of Dr. Bonnie Tanner, University of Kentucky,
Assistant Director of Cooperative Extension Service for
Family and Consumer Sciences

4 cups mashed baked sweet potatoes
1/2 cup (1 stick) butter
2 cups sugar
4 eggs, beaten
1/8 teaspoon salt
2 teaspoons vanilla extract

1/2 cup milk
1 (20-ounce) can crushed pineapple
1/2 cup flour
1/2 cup (1 stick) butter
1 cup sugar
2 eggs, beaten

Combine the sweet potatoes, 1/2 cup butter, 2 cups sugar, 4 eggs, salt, vanilla and milk in a mixing bowl and mix well. Spoon into a 2-quart baking dish.

Combine the pineapple, flour, 1/2 cup butter, 1 cup sugar and 2 eggs in a saucepan and mix well. Cook until thickened, stirring constantly. Spread over the sweet potato mixture. Bake at 350 degrees for 35 minutes or until firm. *Yield: 8 servings.*

Sweet Potato Custard Pie

3 cups sliced cooked sweet potatoes
1 cup sugar
2 eggs
1 cup milk

1/2 cup (1 stick) margarine or butter
1 tablespoon vanilla extract
1/2 cup raisins or coconut (optional)
2 unbaked (9-inch) pie shells

Combine the sweet potatoes, sugar, eggs, milk, margarine and vanilla in a mixing bowl and mix well. Stir in the raisins. Spoon into the pie shells. Bake at 350 degrees for 30 minutes or until the crust is brown. *Yield: 16 servings.*

Taylor Made Salsa

Recipe courtesy of Taylor Snedegar, Chef, Café Jennifer, Lexington

1 or 2 ripe jalapeño chiles, or
    to taste
3 pounds ripe tomatoes, chopped
1/2 cup finely chopped red onion

1/2 cup firmly packed cilantro leaves,
    coarsely chopped
1 tablespoon celery salt
2 tablespoons fresh lime juice

Chop the jalapeño chiles finely, discarding the stems and seeds. Combine the tomatoes, jalapeño chiles, onion, cilantro, celery salt and lime juice in a 4-quart nonmetal bowl and mix well. Chill, covered, for 1 to 2 hours before serving. *Yield: 12 servings.*

Tomato and Chipotle Salsa

Recipe courtesy of John Foster, Chef, Harvest Restaurant, Lexington

8 tomatoes, chopped
2 red bell peppers, chopped
2 green bell peppers, chopped
1 yellow onion, chopped
2 ounces fresh cilantro, chopped
3 chipotle chiles, chopped
Juice of 4 limes

Juice of 1 lemon
1 teaspoon cumin
1 teaspoon red chili powder
1 tablespoon chopped garlic
2 tablespoons olive oil
Salt to taste

Combine the tomatoes, bell peppers and onion in a large bowl and mix well. Add the cilantro, chipotle chiles, lime juice, lemon juice, cumin, chili powder, garlic and olive oil and mix well. Season with salt to taste. Chill, covered, until ready to serve. Serve with chips or quesadillas. *Yield: 12 servings.*

Fresh Tomato and Basil Ring

8 ounces mozzarella cheese, sliced
6 medium tomatoes, sliced
1/2 cup chopped fresh basil leaves

2 tablespoons olive oil
Salt and freshly ground pepper
    to taste

Alternate the cheese and tomatoes in concentric circles in a 9-inch glass pie plate. Sprinkle with the basil, olive oil, salt and pepper. Bake at 325 degrees for 5 minutes or until the cheese begins to melt. Serve warm. (This is a summertime favorite. Just go to your garden and gather fresh tomatoes and basil.) *Yield: 6 servings.*

Fayette Fried Green Tomatoes

1/2 cup flour
1/2 cup cornmeal
1/2 teaspoon salt

1/8 teaspoon pepper
6 green tomatoes
1/4 cup bacon drippings

Mix the flour, cornmeal, salt and pepper in a shallow dish. Cut the tomatoes into slices 1/2 inch thick. Dredge in the flour mixture to coat. Fry in the hot bacon drippings until golden brown, turning once. *Yield: 6 servings.*

This large garden in Warren County was typical for many Kentucky families in the 1930s. Then as now, the University of Kentucky provides research-based information to families through County Extension Agents and their programs.

Tomato Pesto Tart

1 refrigerator pie pastry
2 cups (8 ounces) shredded
   mozzarella cheese
5 plum tomatoes, sliced
1/2 cup mayonnaise

1/4 cup grated Parmesan cheese
2 tablespoons Basil Pesto (below)
1/2 teaspoon pepper
3 tablespoons chopped fresh basil

Unfold the pastry on a lightly greased pizza pan. Roll into a 12-inch circle. Brush the outer edge with water. Fold the edge up and crimp. Prick the bottom with a fork. Bake at 425 degrees for 8 to 10 minutes. Remove from the oven. Reduce the oven temperature to 375 degrees.

Sprinkle the crust with half the mozzarella cheese. Let stand for 15 minutes to cool. Arrange the tomatoes over the mozzarella cheese. Combine the remaining mozzarella cheese, mayonnaise, Parmesan cheese, 2 tablespoons Basil Pesto and pepper in a bowl and mix well. Spread over the tomato slices. Bake for 20 to 25 minutes. Remove from the oven. Sprinkle with the basil. *Yield: 8 servings.*

Basil Pesto

1 1/2 cups packed fresh basil leaves
1 large garlic clove
2 tablespoons walnuts, almonds or
   pine nuts
6 tablespoons packed chopped fresh
   parsley

2 tablespoons grated Parmesan
   cheese
2 tablespoons olive oil
2 tablespoons butter, melted
1/4 teaspoon salt

Process the basil, garlic, walnuts, parsley, Parmesan cheese, olive oil, butter and salt in a food processor fitted with the knife blade until smooth. Store, covered, in an airtight container in the refrigerator. *Yield: 8 (2-tablespoon) servings.*

Tomato Jam

Kentucky Fresh

Recipe courtesy of Joe Castro, Chef, Camberley Brown, Louisville

10 pounds tomatoes, peeled and
    seeded
7 cups (3½ pounds) sugar

1 tablespoon lemon juice
1 teaspoon cinnamon

Chop the tomatoes coarsely into 1-inch pieces and place in a stainless steel stockpot. Add the sugar, lemon juice and cinnamon and mix well. Bring to a boil over medium-high heat. Cook until a smooth textured mass forms, whisking frequently. Remove from the heat to cool. Serve with Stilton cheese, apples and crusty bread or biscuits. *Yield: 10 servings.*

Oven-Fried Zucchini

3 tablespoons herb-seasoned bread
    crumbs
1 tablespoon grated Parmesan cheese
¼ teaspoon salt or garlic salt
⅛ teaspoon pepper

2 medium unpeeled zucchini or
    yellow squash
2 teaspoons vegetable oil
2 tablespoons water

Mix the bread crumbs, Parmesan cheese, salt and pepper together on a sheet of waxed paper. Cut the zucchini into quarters lengthwise. Cut each quarter into halves or thirds. Place in a plastic bag and add the oil and water. Close the bag and shake until the zucchini is lightly coated. Roll each in the bread crumb mixture until lightly coated. Arrange in a single layer on a baking sheet sprayed liberally with nonstick cooking spray. Bake at 475 degrees for 7 minutes or until brown. *Yield: 4 servings.*

Zucchini with Salsa

4 medium zucchini, sliced
3 medium tomatoes, chopped
1 medium onion, chopped
3 green onions, sliced
2 jalapeño chiles, seeded and minced

2 garlic cloves, minced
1 tablespoon fresh cilantro or parsley,
   minced
Salt and pepper to taste

Divide the zucchini between two 18×20-inch pieces of heavy-duty foil. Combine the tomatoes, onion, green onions, jalapeño chiles, garlic, cilantro, salt and pepper in a bowl and mix well. Spoon over the zucchini. Fold the foil around the zucchini and seal tightly. Place on a grill rack. Grill, covered, over indirect heat for 15 to 20 minutes or until tender. (You may also bake in a 400-degree oven for 20 minutes. When cutting and seeding hot chiles, use rubber or plastic gloves to protect your hands and avoid touching your face.) *Yield: 10 servings.*

Cobell Zucchini Combo

3 medium zucchini or yellow squash,
   sliced
2 cups sliced mushrooms
$1/4$ teaspoon garlic powder

$1/2$ teaspoon salt
$1/4$ cup ($1/2$ stick) margarine
2 medium tomatoes, cut into wedges
$1/4$ cup grated Parmesan cheese

Mix the zucchini and mushrooms in a $1^1/2$-quart microwave-safe dish. Sprinkle with garlic powder and salt. Dot with the margarine. Microwave, covered, on High for 7 to 8 minutes or until tender. Stir in the tomatoes and cheese. Microwave, covered, for 2 to 3 minutes or until the cheese is melted. *Yield: 6 servings.*

ZUCCHINI TOMATO SAUTÉ OVER SPAGHETTI

1 garlic clove
1 teaspoon salt
1 tablespoon butter
3 tablespoons olive oil
6 medium zucchini, sliced
1 small onion, sliced
1/4 teaspoon basil

1/4 teaspoon oregano
3 fresh tomatoes, peeled and cut into
  eighths
4 cups cooked spaghetti or pasta of
  choice
2 tablespoons grated Parmesan
  cheese

Mash the garlic with the salt in a bowl. Melt half the butter with half the olive oil in a skillet. Add the zucchini, onion, basil, oregano and garlic mixture. Sauté for 10 to 15 minutes.

Cook the tomatoes in the remaining butter and olive oil in a saucepan for 10 minutes. Add to the zucchini mixture and mix well. Simmer for 10 minutes. Pour over the hot cooked spaghetti in a large bowl. Sprinkle with the Parmesan cheese. *Yield: 8 servings.*

ZUCCHINI RELISH

10 cups grated zucchini
4 onions, chopped
5 tablespoons salt
2 1/2 cups vinegar
6 cups sugar
2 tablespoons celery seeds

1/2 teaspoon pepper
1 teaspoon nutmeg
1 teaspoon dry mustard
1 teaspoon turmeric
5 medium green bell peppers, grated

Mix the zucchini, onions and salt in a bowl. Let stand for 12 hours. Rinse in cold water and drain thoroughly.

Mix the vinegar, sugar, celery seeds, pepper, nutmeg, dry mustard, turmeric and bell peppers in a bowl. Combine with the zucchini mixture in a large saucepan. Cook over medium heat for 30 minutes, stirring frequently. Do not boil. Pack into sterilized 1/2-pint jars, leaving 1/2 inch headspace; seal with 2-piece lids. Process in a boiling water bath for 10 minutes. (Great served with chicken or pork.) *Yield: 24 servings.*

ZUCCHINI BREAD

3 eggs
$^1/_2$ cup applesauce
$^1/_2$ cup vegetable oil
1 cup sugar
1 teaspoon vanilla extract
2 cups finely shredded zucchini
$1^1/_3$ cups all-purpose flour
1 cup whole wheat flour

$^1/_2$ cup wheat germ
1 teaspoon salt
2 teaspoons nutmeg, or $^3/_4$ teaspoon
    freshly ground nutmeg
1 teaspoon baking soda
$^1/_2$ teaspoon baking powder
2 tablespoons grated orange zest
$^1/_2$ cup chopped walnuts

Line two 5×8-inch loaf pans with doubled waxed paper. Spray with nonstick cooking spray. Beat the eggs, applesauce, oil, sugar, vanilla and zucchini in a mixing bowl. Add the all-purpose flour, whole wheat flour, wheat germ, salt, nutmeg, baking soda, baking powder and orange zest and mix well. Stir in the walnuts. Fill each loaf pan $^2/_3$ full. Bake at 350 degrees for 1 hour. Invert onto wire racks to cool. (This bread freezes well.) *Yield: 24 servings.*

CHOCOLATE ZUCCHINI CAKE

3 cups flour
1 teaspoon baking soda
$1^1/_2$ teaspoons baking powder
1 teaspoon salt
4 eggs
$1^1/_2$ cups vegetable oil

3 cups sugar
5 tablespoons baking cocoa
3 cups finely grated zucchini
3 ounces cream cheese, softened
$^1/_4$ cup ($^1/_2$ stick) butter, softened
2 cups confectioners' sugar

Sift the flour, baking soda, baking powder and salt together. Beat the eggs in a mixing bowl until pale yellow. Add the oil, sugar, baking cocoa and zucchini and mix well. Add the flour mixture and mix well. Spoon into a well-greased 9×13-inch cake pan. Bake at 350 degrees for 1 hour. Cool in the pan on a wire rack. Beat the cream cheese and butter in a mixing bowl until smooth and creamy. Add the confectioners' sugar and beat well. (You may add a small amount of milk if needed for the desired consistency.) Spread over the top of the cake. *Yield: 12 servings.*

Vegetable Chowder

3 cups chopped peeled potatoes
2¹/₂ cups chopped broccoli
³/₄ cup chopped onion
1 cup grated carrots
2 ribs celery, chopped
4 teaspoons chicken bouillon
   granules
3 to 4 cups water

³/₄ cup (1¹/₂ sticks) margarine
³/₄ cup flour
4 cups milk
1 teaspoon salt
¹/₄ teaspoon pepper
1 cup (4 ounces) shredded Cheddar
   cheese

Combine the potatoes, broccoli, onion, carrots, celery, bouillon granules and water in a stockpot and mix well. Bring to a boil and reduce the heat. Simmer for 20 minutes or until the vegetables are tender.

Melt the margarine in a saucepan. Stir in the flour. Cook over medium heat for 2 minutes, stirring constantly. Whisk in the milk, salt and pepper. Bring to a boil. Boil for 2 minutes, stirring constantly. Add to the vegetable mixture. Simmer for 10 minutes. Stir in the cheese. Heat just until melted. *Yield: 12 servings.*

Vegetable Pie

1 unbaked (9-inch) deep-dish pie
   shell
2 cups chopped yellow squash
1 medium green bell pepper,
   chopped
1 medium onion, chopped

2 tablespoons margarine
1 medium tomato, sliced
1 cup (4 ounces) shredded
   mozzarella cheese
¹/₂ cup mayonnaise-type salad
   dressing

Bake the pie shell at 325 degrees for 10 minutes. Remove from the oven to cool.

Sauté the squash, bell pepper and onion in the margarine in a skillet until tender. Layer the tomato slices in the prebaked piecrust. Cover with the sautéed vegetables. Mix the cheese and salad dressing in a bowl. Spoon over the vegetables to cover. Bake for 45 minutes. Let stand for 5 minutes before serving. *Yield: 8 servings.*

DOUBLE APPLE SALAD

1 Red Delicious apple, chopped
1 Golden Delicious apple, chopped
1 teaspoon lemon juice
1 (20-ounce) can pineapple chunks, drained
1 cup miniature marshmallows
$^2/_3$ cup flaked coconut
$^1/_2$ cup chopped walnuts
$^1/_4$ cup raisins
$^1/_4$ cup mayonnaise
2 tablespoons chopped celery

Toss the apples with the lemon juice in a bowl. Add the pineapple, marshmallows, coconut, walnuts, raisins, mayonnaise and celery and mix well. Chill, covered, for 1 hour or longer. *Yield: 10 servings.*

MAYS LICK APPLE SALAD

1 (8-ounce) can crushed pineapple
$^1/_2$ cup sugar
1 (3-ounce) package lemon gelatin
8 ounces cream cheese, softened
1 cup chopped unpeeled apple
$^1/_2$ to 1 cup chopped pecans
1 cup chopped celery
1 cup whipped topping

Bring the undrained pineapple and sugar to a boil in a saucepan. Boil for 3 minutes. Add the gelatin. Cook until the gelatin is dissolved, stirring constantly. Add the cream cheese and mix well. Remove from the heat to cool. Fold in the apple, pecans, celery and whipped topping. Spoon into a 9×9-inch dish. Chill until firm. Cut into squares to serve. *Yield: 9 servings.*

APPLE CIDER PANCAKES

$1/4$ cup rolled oats
1 cup pancake mix
$3/4$ cup apple cider
$1/2$ cup shredded apples (optional)
$1/4$ teaspoon cinnamon

Combine the oats, pancake mix and apple cider in a bowl and mix well. Stir in the apples and cinnamon. Pour less than $1/4$ cup of the batter at a time onto a hot griddle sprayed with nonstick cooking spray. Cook for 1 to $1^1/2$ minutes per side or until golden brown. *Yield: 4 servings.*

WOODFORD SLOW COOKER APPLE BUTTER

$1/4$ bushel or 12 pounds fall apples
4 cups sugar
Cinnamon and nutmeg to taste

Core and cut the unpeeled apples into quarters. Cook in a small amount of water in a large saucepan until soft. Cool slightly. Purée in a blender, food processor or food mill. Pour into a slow cooker. Stir in the sugar. Cook on Low for 8 to 10 hours. Stir in the cinnamon and nutmeg. Cook for 2 hours. Ladle into 15 hot sterilized $1/2$-pint jars, leaving $1/4$ inch headspace; seal with 2-piece lids. Process in a boiling water bath for 10 minutes. *Yield: 60 servings.*

APPLE CELEBRATIONS

During the fall harvest season, the goodness of the crisp juicy apple is celebrated all across the state. In 1961 Johnson County held its first Kentucky Apple Festival, and this annual event draws over 100,000. Join the Apple Fest in Trimble County or witness the community making a gigantic apple pie during special activities in Casey County. If you want to sample fresh apple cider or warm fried pies or pick your own apples, visit one of the many orchards like Haney's Appledale Farm in Nancy, Jackson's Orchard in Bowling Green, Garrett's Orchard in Versailles, or High Hill Orchard in Henderson.

WOODFORD MULLED CIDER

4 cups (1 quart) apple cider　　5 whole cloves
1 stick cinnamon　　　　　　　　 1/4 cup packed brown sugar

Combine the apple cider, cinnamon stick, cloves and brown sugar in a saucepan and mix well. Simmer for 15 minutes. Do not boil. Serve hot. *Yield: 8 servings.*

BEDA BROWN BETTY

4 cups 1/2-inch bread cubes　　　　 1/4 teaspoon nutmeg
6 tablespoons margarine, melted　　 1/8 teaspoon salt
3/4 cup packed brown sugar　　　　　4 cups chopped peeled cooking
1/2 teaspoon cinnamon　　　　　　　　　apples

Mix the bread cubes, margarine, brown sugar, cinnamon, nutmeg and salt in a bowl. Alternate layers of the bread mixture and apples in a slow cooker. Cook, covered, on High for 1 1/2 to 2 1/2 hours or until the apples are tender. Serve alone or with a scoop of vanilla ice cream. *Yield: 4 servings.*

Home food preservation was often a community event in the 1930s. Families shared produce, as well as equipment, and County Extension Agents, known as Home Demonstration Agents, demonstrated proper techniques. These ladies from Holmes Mill Community Canning project show the "before" produce which would soon be placed into canning jars and stored until fall and winter.

SMITH GROVE APPLE MACAROONS

½ cup flour

1 teaspoon baking powder

1 teaspoon salt

2 tablespoons butter or margarine, softened

½ cup sugar

1 egg

½ cup shredded coconut

4 tart apples, sliced

Sift the flour, baking powder and salt together. Cream the butter and sugar in a mixing bowl until light and fluffy. Add the egg and beat well. Add the flour mixture and beat well. Stir in the coconut.

Layer the apples in a greased 9-inch deep-dish pie plate. Pour the batter over the apples. Bake at 375 degrees for 35 minutes or until the apples are tender. Serve warm or cold with whipped cream or your favorite sauce.
Yield: 8 servings.

APPLE NUT PUDDING

¾ cup sifted flour

1 teaspoon baking soda

¾ teaspoon salt

½ teaspoon cinnamon

¼ teaspoon nutmeg

2 eggs

¾ cup sugar

1 teaspoon almond extract

¾ cup chopped pecans

1½ cups chopped apples

Sift the sifted flour with the baking soda, salt, cinnamon and nutmeg. Beat the eggs in a mixing bowl until light. Add the sugar gradually, beating constantly. Add the flour mixture and mix well. Beat in the almond extract. Add the pecans and apples and mix well. Spoon into a well-greased 8×8-inch baking pan. Bake at 325 degrees for 40 to 45 minutes. Serve with whipped cream or ice cream.
Yield: 6 servings.

Fresh Apple Cake with Brown Sugar Icing

3 cups flour
1 teaspoon baking soda
1 teaspoon baking powder
$1/2$ teaspoon salt
2 cups sugar
3 cups sliced apples
$1^1/2$ cups chopped pecans
$1^1/2$ cups vegetable oil
3 eggs
1 teaspoon vanilla extract
Brown Sugar Icing (below)

Mix the flour, baking soda, baking powder, salt and sugar in a large bowl. Add the apples, pecans, oil, eggs and vanilla and mix well. Spoon into a bundt pan sprayed with nonstick cooking spray. Bake at 350 degrees for 1 hour. Cool in the pan for 10 minutes. Invert onto a cake plate. Spoon Brown Sugar Icing over the cake, spooning any icing that runs to the plate back onto the cake until the icing sticks. *Yield: 24 servings.*

Brown Sugar Icing

1 cup packed light brown sugar
$1/2$ cup (1 stick) margarine
$1/4$ cup milk
1 teaspoon vanilla extract

Mix the brown sugar, margarine and milk in a 1-quart saucepan. Bring to a boil. Boil for 4 minutes. Remove from the heat. Stir in the vanilla. *Yield: 24 servings.*

JOHNSON COUNTY APPLE LAYER CAKE WITH COCONUT PECAN FROSTING

4 cups finely chopped peeled apples
1³/₄ cups sugar
3 cups flour
¹/₂ teaspoon salt
1¹/₂ teaspoons baking soda

2 eggs, beaten
³/₄ cup vegetable oil
1 teaspoon vanilla extract
¹/₄ teaspoon cinnamon
Coconut Pecan Frosting (below)

Toss the apples with the sugar in a mixing bowl. Let stand for 30 minutes. Add the flour, salt and baking soda. Beat for 1 minute. Add the eggs, oil, vanilla and cinnamon. Beat at medium speed for 3 minutes. Spoon into 2 or 3 greased 9-inch cake pans. Bake at 350 degrees for 25 minutes. Invert onto wire racks to cool. Spread the Coconut Pecan Frosting between the layers and over the top and side of the cake. *Yield: 12 servings.*

COCONUT PECAN FROSTING

1¹/₂ cups sugar
1 (5-ounce) can evaporated milk
¹/₂ cup (1 stick) butter or margarine

¹/₂ cup chopped pecans
1 cup flaked coconut
1 teaspoon vanilla extract

Combine the sugar and evaporated milk in a saucepan. Cook over medium heat until 240 degrees on a candy thermometer, soft-ball stage, stirring constantly. Add the butter, pecans, coconut and vanilla and stir until the butter melts. *Yield: 12 servings.*

Edna Smith's Old-Fashioned Stack Cake with Apple Filling

2 cups sugar	3 eggs
1 cup shortening	$1/2$ teaspoon salt
2 teaspoons baking soda	$1/2$ teaspoon vanilla extract
1 cup buttermilk	1 cup (about) flour
4 cups flour	Apple Filling (below)

Cream the sugar and shortening in a mixing bowl until light and fluffy. Dissolve the baking soda in the buttermilk. Add the buttermilk and 4 cups flour alternately to the creamed mixture, beating well after each addition. Beat in the eggs 1 at a time. Add the salt and vanilla and mix well. Place the dough on a lightly floured surface. Knead in enough of the 1 cup flour to form a dough with a biscuit-like consistency. Divide the dough into 7 equal portions. Shape each portion into a ball. Place each ball in a greased 9-inch cake pan and press to line the bottom of the pan. Bake at 350 degrees for 15 minutes. (You may cook each layer on a hot greased 9-inch skillet or griddle.) Invert onto wire racks to cool. Spread Apple Filling between each layer and over the top of the cake. Let stand, covered, for 1 to 2 days before serving for the best flavor. *Yield: 12 servings.*

Apple Filling

1 quart dried apples	1 teaspoon allspice
$1^1/2$ to 2 cups sugar	1 teaspoon cinnamon

Soak the apples in water to cover in a bowl for 8 to 12 hours. Pour into a saucepan. Cook over low heat until the apples are very tender, stirring frequently and adding as little additional water as possible to keep from scorching. Remove from the heat. Mash the apple mixture. Stir in the sugar, allspice and cinnamon. Let stand until cool. *Yield: 12 servings.*

Edna Smith's Old-Fashioned Stack Cake with Strawberry Filling

1 recipe Old-Fashioned Stack Cake
    (page 170)
2 pints fresh strawberries
2 cups sugar

1/4 cup cornstarch
2 cups water
3 tablespoons strawberry gelatin

Prepare the cake layers as directed on page 170. Rinse the strawberries and remove the stems; drain. Reserve several whole strawberries for the top. Mash the remaining strawberries in a bowl to make about 2 cups.

Combine the sugar, cornstarch and water in a saucepan and mix well. Cook over medium heat until thick and clear. Remove from the heat. Stir in the gelatin. Cool slightly. Stir in the mashed strawberries. Chill, covered, in the refrigerator for 1 hour or place in the freezer for 30 minutes.

Place 1 cake layer in a serving dish with at least a 1-inch side. Spoon some of the strawberry filling over the layer so that some of the filling drizzles down the edge. Continue stacking with the remaining cake layers and strawberry filling, spooning the remaining strawberry filling over the top layer. Arrange the reserved strawberries on the top. Chill until the filling is set and the layers are moistened. *Yield: 12 servings.*

DRIED APPLE STACK CAKE

6 cups flour, sifted
1 teaspoon baking soda
1 tablespoon baking powder
1/2 teaspoon salt
1 teaspoon cinnamon
1/2 teaspoon nutmeg
13/4 cups sugar

1 cup (2 sticks) butter, softened, or 1
    cup shortening
1/4 cup sorghum or brown sugar
2 eggs
1 teaspoon vanilla extract
1/2 cup buttermilk
Dried Apple Filling (below)

Sift the sifted flour, baking soda, baking powder, salt, cinnamon and nutmeg together. Cream the sugar and butter in a mixing bowl until light and fluffy. Add the sorghum, eggs and vanilla and beat well. Add the flour mixture alternately with the buttermilk, beating well after each addition. Divide the dough into 6 equal portions. Shape each portion into a ball. Place each ball in the middle of a greased and floured 9-inch cake pan. Pat the dough to the edge of the pan, turning the pan so the dough will be evenly distributed. Bake at 375 degrees for 10 to 12 minutes or until the top is light brown. Cool in the pans for 2 minutes. Remove the layers from the pans.

Place 1 cake layer on a cake plate. Spread hot Dried Apple Filling over the layer. Continue stacking the remaining cake layers and spreading Dried Apple Filling between the layers until all layers are used. Cover and let stand for 10 to 12 hours before serving. *Yield: 12 servings.*

DRIED APPLE FILLING

1 pound home-dried apples
1 cup sugar
1/2 cup packed brown sugar

1/2 teaspoon nutmeg
2 teaspoons cinnamon
1/2 teaspoon ground cloves

Rinse the dried apples. Place in a large saucepan and cover with water. Cook until the apples are tender. Mash the apples to a spreading consistency. Add the sugar, brown sugar, nutmeg, cinnamon and cloves and mix well. (You may pre-soak the dried apples and cook in the soaking water. You may substitute cooked apples or applesauce for 1/4 of the cooked dried apples.) *Yield: 12 servings.*

OLD-FASHIONED PASTRY APPLE BARS

2$\frac{1}{2}$ cups sifted flour
1 teaspoon salt
1 cup shortening
1 egg yolk
$\frac{1}{2}$ cup plus 3$\frac{1}{2}$ teaspoons (about) milk
1 cup cornflakes
8 to 10 tart apples, peeled and sliced
1 cup sugar
1 teaspoon cinnamon
1 egg white
1 tablespoon (about) milk
1 cup confectioners' sugar
$\frac{1}{2}$ teaspoon vanilla extract

Mix the flour and salt in a medium bowl. Cut in the shortening until crumbly.
Beat the egg yolk in a measuring cup. Add enough of the $\frac{1}{2}$ cup plus
3$\frac{1}{2}$ teaspoons milk to measure $\frac{2}{3}$ cup and mix well. Add to the flour mixture
and mix well. Divide the dough into 2 equal portions. Roll each portion into a
12×17-inch rectangle on a floured surface. Line a 10×15-inch baking pan with
1 portion of the pastry. Sprinkle with the cornflakes. Top with the apples.
Sprinkle with a mixture of the sugar and cinnamon. Top with the remaining
pastry, sealing the edges and cutting vents. Beat the egg white in a bowl until
frothy. Brush over the pastry. Bake at 375 degrees for 50 minutes.

Blend 1 tablespoon milk, confectioners' sugar and vanilla in a bowl until
smooth. Drizzle over the warm pastry. Cut into bars. (You may freeze the bars in
individual portions for a quick breakfast on the run.) *Yield: 20 servings.*

*Apples are one of Kentucky's favorite fruits. They supply vitamins and
minerals plus fiber. An average apple has about 80 calories.*

OLLIE PEARL'S STACKED HAND APPLE PIES

8 refrigerator or homemade pie pastries	1/2 teaspoon nutmeg
	1/2 teaspoon cinnamon
2 1/2 cups reconstituted dried apples	1 tablespoon lemon juice
3/4 cup sugar	2 teaspoons sugar (crust topping)

Grease four 8-inch tart pans with vegetable oil. Roll each pastry into a 9 inch circle. Fit half the pastries into the prepared tart pans. Mix the reconstituted apples with 3/4 cup sugar, nutmeg, cinnamon and lemon juice. Spread about 1/2 cup of the apple mixture about 1/4 inch thick in the prepared pans. Top with the remaining pastry, trimming and fluting the edge. Prick the tops with a fork. Sprinkle each with 1/2 teaspoon sugar. Bake at 375 degrees for 15 to 20 minutes or until light brown and the edges shrink from the pans. Cool briefly. Remove the pies from the pans, stacking on top of each other on a serving plate. To serve, cut a wedge through all layers of the pies. Eat by picking up one layer at a time. Thus, the name, a "hand pie." *Yield: 24 servings.*

Whether dried in the backyard or in a sunny window as grandmother did or in today's dehydrators, dried apples are a part of Kentucky's food heritage. They can be eaten as a snack or reconstituted for a variety of Kentucky favorites like stack cake, fried pies, or Ollie Pearl's Stacked Hand Pies.

Making Ollie Pearl's Pies

TRAVELLERS REST APPLE FREEZER PIE

4 cups sliced apples
1/2 cup sugar
1/2 teaspoon cinnamon
1 (9-inch) frozen pie shell

3/4 cup flour
1/2 cup sugar
1/3 cup plus 2 tablespoons butter

Toss the apples, 1/2 cup sugar and cinnamon together in a bowl. Place in the frozen pie shell. Mix the flour and 1/2 cup sugar in a bowl. Cut in 1/3 cup of the butter until crumbly. Sprinkle over the apples. Cut 2 tablespoons of the butter into pats and place on top of the crumbled mixture. Place in a 1-gallon freezer bag. Freeze until ready to bake. Remove from the freezer bag. Bake at 450 degrees for 10 minutes. Reduce the oven temperature to 350 degrees. Bake for 40 minutes longer. *Yield: 6 servings.*

FRESH BLACKBERRY CAKE

3 cups flour
2 teaspoons baking soda
2 teaspoons ground cloves
1 1/2 teaspoons cinnamon
1 1/2 teaspoons allspice
1 cup (2 sticks) margarine, softened

2 cups sugar
3 eggs
2 cups undrained blackberries
1 cup chopped pecans
1 cup raisins (optional)

Sift the flour, baking soda, cloves, cinnamon and allspice together. Cream the margarine and sugar in a mixing bowl until light and fluffy. Add the eggs 1 at a time, beating well after each addition. Add the flour mixture gradually, beating well after each addition. Add the undrained blackberries, pecans and raisins and mix well. Pour into a greased and floured tube pan. Bake at 350 degrees for 50 to 60 minutes or until the cake tests done. (This cake is great for breakfast or brunch. You may frost with caramel or butter frosting and serve for dessert. The cake can also be frozen for a short period. For a sweeter taste, you may add 1/2 cup sugar to the blackberries and let stand for 30 minutes before adding to the batter.) *Yield: 24 servings.*

Kentucky Culture

WILD BLACKBERRIES

Wild blackberries grow throughout Kentucky. For generations, Kentucky families have picked and enjoyed their sweet flavor. In addition to pies and cobblers, blackberries were cooked into jams and jellies. Fresh jams were used on homemade biscuits but, as the jam aged, it was used more often in cakes. This tradition continues in many Kentucky families today.

Washington Jam Cake with Brown Sugar Icing

3 cups flour
1 tablespoon cinnamon
2 teaspoons allspice
2 teaspoons nutmeg
2 tablespoons baking cocoa
1/8 teaspoon salt
1 teaspoon baking soda

1 cup buttermilk
4 eggs
1 cup vegetable oil
2 cups sugar
1 cup blackberry jam
Brown Sugar Icing (below)

Sift the flour, cinnamon, allspice, nutmeg, baking cocoa and salt together. Dissolve the baking soda in the buttermilk. Beat the eggs lightly in a mixing bowl. Add the oil and sugar and beat well. Add the buttermilk and mix well. Fold in the flour mixture. Fold in the jam. Pour into 2 greased and floured 8-inch cake pans. Bake at 350 degrees for 30 minutes or until a wooden pick inserted near the center comes out clean. Spread Brown Sugar Icing between the layers and over the top and side of the cake. *Yield: 12 servings.*

Brown Sugar Icing

1/2 cup (1 stick) butter
1 cup packed brown sugar
1/4 cup milk

1 teaspoon vanilla extract
13/4 to 2 cups confectioners' sugar

Bring the butter and brown sugar to a boil in a saucepan over medium heat. Boil for 2 minutes, stirring constantly. Remove from the heat. Stir in the milk. Return to the heat and bring to a boil. Remove from the heat and cool. Stir in the vanilla and enough of the confectioners' sugar to make of a spreading consistency. *Yield: 12 servings.*

Berry Almond Streusel

4 cups blueberries
4 cups blackberries
1/4 cup cornstarch
1/4 cup packed brown sugar
1/2 cup orange juice
2 tablespoons orange zest
3/4 cup flour

1/2 cup packed brown sugar
1/2 teaspoon salt
4 1/2 tablespoons butter, cut into
   pieces
3/4 cup rolled oats
1/3 cup sliced almonds

Combine the blueberries, blackberries, cornstarch, 1/4 cup brown sugar, orange juice and orange zest in a large mixing bowl and mix gently with a wooden spoon. Spoon into a 9×13-inch baking pan. Pulse the flour, 1/2 cup brown sugar and salt in a food processor twice or until mixed. Add the butter and pulse 6 times or until the mixture resembles coarse meal. Add the oats and almonds and pulse twice. Sprinkle over the berry mixture. Bake at 350 degrees for 30 minutes or until bubbly and light brown. *Yield: 12 servings.*

Blueberry Spice Jam

2 1/2 pints ripe blueberries
1 tablespoon lemon juice
1/2 teaspoon nutmeg or cinnamon
3/4 cup water

1 (1 3/4-ounce) package powdered
   pectin
5 1/2 cups sugar

Rinse the blueberries. Crush the blueberries 1 layer at a time in a saucepan. Add the lemon juice, nutmeg and water and mix well. Stir in the pectin. Bring to a full rolling boil over high heat, stirring frequently. Add the sugar. Return to a rolling boil. Boil for 1 minute, stirring constantly. Remove from the heat. Skim off the foam quickly. Ladle into 5 sterilized 1/2-pint jars, leaving 1/4 inch headspace; seal with 2-piece lids. Process in a boiling water bath for 10 minutes. *Yield: 60 servings.*

Safe Home Canning

There are two ways to safely can foods: the boiling water method and the pressure canner method. Use the boiling water bath for high acid foods, such as fruits, tomatoes, pickles, jams, jellies, and preserves. This method means immersing filled and lidded jars into a large pot of boiling water, covered and heated for a specified time.

Pressure canning is the only recommended method for low acid foods, including vegetables, meats, poultry, and fish. Filled and lidded jars are placed in the pressure canner with 2 to 3 inches of water, covered and heated to 240 degrees F. This is only achieved by creating 10 to 15 pounds of pressure and is necessary to kill botulism spores. Low acid home canned foods should be boiled for 13 minutes before eating in order to destroy any toxins that might be present.

HIGH BRIDGE BLUEBERRY CRISP

4 cups fresh blueberries
3/4 cup packed brown sugar
1/2 cup self-rising or all-purpose flour
1/2 cup rolled oats

3/4 teaspoon cinnamon
3/4 teaspoon nutmeg
1/3 cup butter or margarine

Grease the bottom and sides of an 8×8-inch baking pan with nonstick cooking spray or butter. Rinse the blueberries and drain. Place in the prepared pan. Mix the brown sugar, flour, oats, cinnamon and nutmeg in a bowl. Cut in the butter until crumbly. Sprinkle over the blueberries. Bake at 375 degrees for 30 minutes or until the top is golden brown. Serve warm alone or topped with ice cream. *Yield: 6 servings.*

BLUEBERRY POUND CAKE

2 cups sugar
1/2 cup (1 stick) lite butter
4 ounces 1/3 less fat cream cheese, softened
3 eggs
1 egg white
2 cups fresh or frozen blueberries

3 cups flour
1 teaspoon baking powder
1/2 teaspoon each baking soda and salt
8 ounces lemon low-fat yogurt
2 teaspoons vanilla extract
1/2 cup confectioners' sugar
4 teaspoons lemon juice

Beat the sugar, butter and cream cheese at medium speed in a mixing bowl for 5 minutes or until blended. Add the eggs and egg white 1 at a time, beating well after each addition. Toss the blueberries and 2 tablespoons of the flour in a small bowl. Mix the remaining flour, baking powder, baking soda and salt together. Add to the cream cheese mixture alternately with the yogurt, beginning and ending with the flour mixture. Fold in the blueberry mixture and vanilla. Pour into a 10-inch tube pan sprayed with nonstick cooking spray. Bake at 350 degrees for 1 hour and 10 minutes or until a wooden pick inserted in the center comes out clean. Cool in the pan for 10 minutes. Invert onto a cake plate. Mix the confectioners' sugar and lemon juice in a small bowl. Drizzle over the warm cake. Cut into slices with a serrated knife. *Yield: 12 servings.*

Blueberry Dessert

10 to 12 slices bread	1 cup sugar
4 cups blueberries	1/4 teaspoon cinnamon
1 cup sugar	1/8 teaspoon nutmeg
1/2 cup (1 stick) butter, melted	1/4 cup (1/2 stick) butter
2 tablespoons flour	1/2 teaspoon vanilla extract

Trim the bread and cut into cubes. Rinse the blueberries and place in a saucepan. Add enough water to almost cover the blueberries. Cook until tender. Remove the blueberries with a slotted spoon to a greased 2 1/2-quart baking dish, reserving the juice in the saucepan. Sprinkle the blueberries with 1 cup sugar. Spread the bread cubes evenly over the top. Drizzle 1/2 cup butter over the bread cubes. Bake at 350 degrees for 45 minutes or until the bread is brown.

Mix the flour, 1 cup sugar, cinnamon and nutmeg in a bowl. Add to the reserved juice in the saucepan. Add 1/4 cup butter. Cook until thickened, stirring constantly. Stir in the vanilla. Pour over the hot blueberry dish. Serve with vanilla ice cream. *Yield: 8 servings.*

Grape Plum Jelly

3 1/2 pounds ripe plums	1 (1 3/4-ounce) package powdered
3 pounds ripe Concord grapes	pectin
1 cup water	8 1/2 cups sugar
1/2 teaspoon butter or margarine	

Wash and pit the plums; do not peel. Crush the plums and grapes thoroughly 1 layer at a time in a saucepan. Add the water. Bring to a boil and cover. Simmer for 10 minutes. Strain the juice through a jelly bag or double layer of cheesecloth, discarding the pulp. Combine 6 1/2 cups of the juice, butter and pectin in a large saucepan. Bring to a hard boil over high heat, stirring constantly. Add the sugar. Return to a full rolling boil. Boil hard for 1 minute, stirring constantly. Remove from the heat. Skim off the foam quickly. Ladle into 10 sterilized 1/2-pint jars, leaving 1/4 inch headspace; seal with 2-piece lids. Process in a boiling water bath for 10 minutes. *Yield: 160 servings.*

Reprocessing Unsealed Jars

If a jar of home canned food fails to seal, remove the lid and check the jar-sealing surface for tiny nicks. If necessary, change the jar, add a new properly prepared lid, and reprocess within 24 hours using the same processing time. Another option is to adjust headspace in unsealed jars to 1 1/2 inch and freeze jars and contents instead of reprocessing. However, make sure jars have straight sides because freezing may crack jars with "shoulders."

Foods in single unsealed jars could be stored in the refrigerator and consumed within several days.

EASY PEACH COBBLER

¹/₂ cup (1 stick) butter
1 cup flour
2 teaspoons baking powder
1 cup sugar

³/₄ cup milk
3 cups peaches or berries
1 cup sugar
¹/₂ cup water

Melt the butter and pour into a baking dish. Mix the flour, baking powder, 1 cup sugar and milk in a bowl. Pour over the melted butter. Spread the peaches over the dough. Mix 1 cup sugar and water in a bowl. Pour over the peaches. Bake at 350 degrees for 45 to 50 minutes. (The dough rises to the top of the peaches and makes a top crust.) *Yield: 8 servings.*

STRAWBERRY RHUBARB JELLY

1¹/₂ pounds red stalks of rhubarb
1¹/₂ quarts ripe strawberries
¹/₂ teaspoon butter or margarine
   (optional)

6 cups sugar
6 ounces liquid pectin

Wash and cut the rhubarb into 1-inch pieces. Process in a food processor until blended or ground. Wash the strawberries and remove the stems. Crush the strawberries 1 layer at a time in a saucepan. Place the rhubarb and strawberries in a jelly bag or double layer of cheesecloth and gently squeeze out the juice, discarding the pulp. Measure 3¹/₂ cups of the juice and pour into a large saucepan. Add the butter and sugar and mix well. Bring to a boil over high heat, stirring constantly. Stir in the pectin immediately. Bring to a full rolling boil. Boil hard for 1 minute, stirring constantly. Remove from the heat. Skim off the foam quickly. Ladle into 7 sterilized ¹/₂-pint jars, leaving ¹/₄ inch headspace; seal with 2-piece lids. Process in a boiling water bath for 10 minutes. *Yield: 120 servings.*

Sunrise Strawberry Pie

²/₃ cup sugar
2 tablespoons cornstarch
1 cup water
¹/₂ (3-ounce) package strawberry gelatin
1 quart strawberries
1 baked (8-inch) pie shell

Combine the sugar, cornstarch and water in a saucepan and mix well. Cook until thickened and clear, stirring constantly. Stir in the gelatin. Pour over the strawberries in a bowl and toss lightly. Spoon into the pie shell. Chill in the refrigerator until set. Serve with whipped cream. *Yield: 8 servings.*

Many families, for an alternative crop, raise and often sell strawberries. How wonderful they are picked ripe and eaten fresh, May until early June.

Strawberry Salsa

6 tablespoons olive oil
2 tablespoons white balsamic vinegar
¹/₂ teaspoon salt
1 pint fresh strawberries, coarsely chopped
8 green onions, chopped
2 pints cherry tomatoes, chopped
¹/₂ cup chopped fresh cilantro

Whisk the olive oil, vinegar and salt in a large bowl. Add the strawberries, green onions, tomatoes and cilantro and toss to coat. Chill, covered, for 1 hour or longer. Serve with tortilla chips. *Yield: 7 servings.*

WILDER WATERMELON SALSA

2 cups chopped fresh watermelon
1 cup chopped Roma tomatoes
1 cucumber, peeled and chopped
$^1/_2$ cup chopped sweet onion
$^1/_2$ cup chopped mint leaves
$^1/_2$ cup red wine vinegar
$^1/_4$ cup sugar
$^1/_2$ teaspoon salt
$^1/_4$ teaspoon pepper

Combine the watermelon, tomatoes, cucumber, onion and mint in a large bowl. Combine the vinegar, sugar, salt and pepper in a small jar with a lid. Seal the jar and shake well until the sugar is dissolved. Pour over the watermelon mixture. Marinate for 30 minutes. Serve over fresh salad greens. *Yield: 12 servings.*

FARMERS' MARKET FRUIT

2 cups water
2 cups sugar
Fresh spearmint leaves to taste
2 cups fresh watermelon balls or chunks
2 cups fresh cantaloupe balls or chunks
2 cups fresh blackberries
2 cups seedless green grapes

Mix the water and sugar in a 2-quart saucepan. Bring to a boil and remove from the heat. Add the spearmint leaves. Let stand until cool. Discard the spearmint leaves. Pour into a bowl. Chill, covered, until ready to serve.

Toss the watermelon, cantaloupe, blackberries and grapes in a large bowl. Spoon into dessert cups. Drizzle with the mint syrup just before serving. *Yield: 6 servings.*

Sensational Spirits, Sips, and Sweets
Bourbon · Wine · Honey · Sorghum

In the 1930s, men joined in the food preserving efforts. These fellows from the Shields Community Canning kitchen work outside the kitchen with the heavy canning equipment. Today men still enjoy making special recipes to preserve for family meals and gifts.

Kentucky honey, sweet sorghum, wine, and bourbon may not always be thought of as basic agricultural commodities, but production is significant to our agricultural economy. These products also play an important role in our food culture and are often found as basic ingredients in both traditional and new Kentucky recipes.

In 2001, honey production from 3,000 colonies of bees totaled 234,000 pounds, up 63 percent from 2000. Retail sales by producers and sales to private processors and co-ops totaled more than a quarter of a million dollars.

Sweet sorghum syrup production dates back to colonial days, and Kentucky is one of eight states producing about 90 percent of the total sweet sorghum. Records show that in 1899, Kentucky raised 21,982 acres, but by 1972 that number had decreased to fewer than 500 acres. Since then acreage has steadily grown, and by 1994 sorghum was worth more than $8 million, with the current acreage estimated to be just over one-half of Kentucky's potential. The term "sorghum molasses" is a colloquial expression often incorrectly applied to sorghum syrup in Kentucky. Molasses is a by-product of the sugar crystallization from sugarcane juice.

There are ten operating wineries in Kentucky, mostly in the central part of the state. However, wine production dates back to 1798, when John James Dufour founded the Kentucky Vineyard Society. Kentucky was the site of the first commercial vineyard in the United States, and by 1860 it was the third largest wine producing state. Production stopped during the American Civil War, and grapevines were ripped from the ground during Prohibition. There was a return to commercial grape production as Kentucky producers diversified operations in the 1990s, and today there are over 280 commercial grape growers.

Kentucky is one of the largest producers of bourbon in the world. This provides a market for the quality grain grown here since—legally—bourbon must contain 51 percent corn, with 75 percent being the average. Some production methods use barley malt and flavor grain such as rye or wheat.

Kentucky Bourbon Nog

²/₃ cup sugar
¹/₃ cup boiling water
4 cups (1 quart) milk
1¹/₂ cups bourbon
1¹/₂ teaspoons vanilla extract
¹/₂ teaspoon nutmeg

Dissolve the sugar in the boiling water in a bowl. Let stand until cool. Add the milk, bourbon, vanilla and nutmeg and whisk until blended. Pour into a pitcher. Chill, covered, in the refrigerator. Serve over ice. Store in the refrigerator.
Yield: 8 servings.

Bourbon Slush

2 cups sugar
2 cups strong brewed tea (made with 4 regular-size tea bags)
7 cups hot water
1 (16-ounce) can frozen orange juice concentrate
1 (12-ounce) can frozen lemonade concentrate
2 cups bourbon
1 liter ginger ale

Combine the sugar, tea, hot water, orange juice concentrate, lemonade concentrate and bourbon in a large freezer container and stir until the sugar is dissolved and the mixture is smooth. Freeze for 3 days or longer.

To serve, spoon half the mixture into a punch bowl and add 4 cups of the ginger ale and stir lightly. Repeat with the remaining ingredients when needed. Garnish with mint sprigs, pineapple chunks and/or cherry on a pick. (You may also serve in individual serving cups by filling half the cup with the frozen mixture and the remaining half with ginger ale and stirring lightly.)
Yield: 30 servings.

GALLREIN FARMS

Gallrein Farms, located about six miles outside of Shelbyville, offers something for everyone. Activities for children include a free petting zoo (with both usual and unusual inhabitants), a pond with ducks and geese to feed, and an observation beehive where you can watch honey being made as the bees work between two plates of glass. In the fall, take a horse-drawn hayride to the pumpkin patch and explore the corn maze.

Adults will appreciate the fresh produce selection, including eighteen varieties of sweet corn, other vegetables, berries, and apples. There's also honey, jams, gourds, dressings, bedding plants, and hanging baskets.

KENTUCKY WINE COOLER

8 cups (2 quarts) white wine
8 cups (2 quarts) ginger ale
1 (6-ounce) can frozen limeade concentrate
2 tablespoons sugar

Combine the wine, ginger ale, limeade concentrate and sugar in a punch bowl and mix well. Serve over ice in individual serving glasses. *Yield: 20 servings.*

HOT SPICED WINE

8 cups (2 quarts) apple juice
8 cups (2 quarts) red wine
2 cinnamon sticks
$^{1}/_{2}$ to 1 cup sugar (optional)

Blend the apple juice and wine in a 5-quart saucepan. Add the cinnamon sticks. Cook until heated through. Do not boil. Stir in the sugar. Pour into a slow cooker, discarding the cinnamon sticks. Cook for 2 hours. Ladle into serving mugs. (Cool any leftovers and cork. Reheat by the cup to serve.) *Yield: 32 servings.*

FRENCH ONION SOUP

¼ cup (½ stick) butter
1 pound onions, thinly sliced
5 cups beef stock or bouillon
8 ounces white wine
1 teaspoon brown sugar

Salt and pepper to taste
6 slices French bread
1 cup (4 ounces) shredded Gruyère
    cheese, or 6 slices Swiss cheese
    or Cheddar cheese

Melt the butter in a large saucepan. Add the onions. Sauté until golden brown. Stir in the beef stock, wine, brown sugar, salt and pepper. Bring to a boil and reduce the heat. Simmer for 40 minutes.

Place the bread on a baking sheet. Bake at 350 degrees until toasted. Sprinkle with the cheese. Bake until the cheese melts.

To serve, ladle the soup into heated soup bowls and float the cheese toast on top. *Yield: 6 servings.*

LEMON CHICKEN BREASTS

3 tablespoons olive oil
4 skinless chicken breasts
1 cup dry white wine
1 teaspoon parsley flakes
½ teaspoon dried whole thyme

¼ teaspoon salt
3 tablespoons lemon juice
¼ teaspoon pepper
¼ teaspoon paprika

Heat the olive oil in a heavy skillet until hot. Add the chicken. Cook for 5 minutes on each side; drain. Place the drained chicken in an 8×8-inch baking dish.

Bring the wine, parsley flakes, thyme and salt to a boil in the skillet. Pour over the chicken. Sprinkle with the lemon juice, pepper and paprika. Bake, covered, at 375 degrees for 35 minutes or until tender and cooked through. *Yield: 4 servings.*

COOKING WITH SORGHUM

Sorghum is one of the oldest natural sweeteners, grown from the sorghum plant. Some folks refer to sorghum as molasses, but that is a colloquial expression often incorrectly applied to sorghum syrup. Molasses is a by-product of the sugar crystallization from sugarcane juice.

Sorghum was the main sweetener used by the early Kentucky settlers, and it provided energy and made otherwise plain foods tasty and nutritious. Pioneer women gave little thought to nutrition, but the sorghum they used in baking, cooking, sweetening drinks, and flavoring meats was providing important nutrients—iron, calcium, potassium, and phosphorous—to their diets. Kentucky cooks continue to enjoy the flavor and sweetness of sorghum.

BOURBONNAISE BARBECUE SAUCE

Recipe courtesy of Graham Waller, Chef, Emmett's, Lexington

1 fifth Kentucky bourbon
1³/₄ cups soy sauce
3 cups ketchup
3 cups Creole mustard
6¹/₂ cups packed brown sugar
1 (4-ounce) can chipotle chiles, minced

Combine the bourbon, soy sauce, ketchup, mustard, brown sugar and chipotle chiles in a heavy stockpot and blend well. Simmer for 2 to 3 hours or until the mixture is reduced by ¹/₃ to ¹/₂, tasting until you enjoy the flavor. Enjoy with pork, chicken or ribs. *Yield: 10 servings.*

Ever since we opened, we have marinated all our pork with this sauce using Kentucky bourbon and spicy chipotle chiles.

BASIC BARBECUE SAUCE

1 cup sorghum
1 cup prepared mustard
1 cup vinegar

Blend the sorghum and mustard in a bowl. Stir in the vinegar. Chill, covered, until ready to use. Use on meat loaves, burgers, ribs, etc., as you would any barbecue sauce. *Yield: 12 servings.*

HONEY MARINADE FOR STEAK

1/2 cup soy sauce
3 tablespoons honey
3 tablespoons vegetable oil
1 tablespoon garlic powder or minced garlic clove
1 teaspoon ginger

Mix the soy sauce, honey, oil, garlic powder and ginger in a sealable plastic bag. Use to marinate steak.

To use, place the steak in the bag and seal. Marinate in the refrigerator for 1 to 8 hours. Drain the steak, discarding the marinade. Grill the steak as desired.
Yield: 15 (1-tablespoon) servings.

HONEY ORANGE GLAZE FOR HAM

1 (6-ounce) can frozen orange juice concentrate
1 3/4 cups water
3/4 cup honey
Salt to taste
1 tablespoon cornstarch

Combine the orange juice concentrate, water, honey and salt in a saucepan and blend well. Dissolve the cornstarch in 1/4 cup of the mixture and return to the saucepan. Cook over medium heat until the mixture thickens and comes to a boil, stirring constantly. Boil for 2 to 3 minutes. Remove from the heat to cool. Use to brush on ham to glaze. (This glaze does not tend to run off as do some other glazes. This recipe makes about 3 1/4 cups.)
Yield: 52 (1-tablespoon) servings.

Store honey at room temperature, not in the refrigerator. If honey crystallizes, a naturally occurring process, place the container of honey in warm water and stir until the crystals dissolve.

Honey French Dressing

½ cup vegetable oil
½ cup vinegar

½ cup honey
½ teaspoon salt

Mix the oil and vinegar in a bowl. Add the honey and salt and beat vigorously. Store, covered, in the refrigerator. Mix well each time before serving over fresh salad greens. *Yield: 12 (2-tablespoon) servings.*

Honey contains a wide variety of vitamins and minerals in trace amounts, including niacin, riboflavin, calcium, copper, iron, potassium, zinc, and more. One tablespoon of honey contains 60 calories, 17 grams of carbohydrate, and 0 fat and protein.

Bourbon Barbecued Beans

4 slices bacon, chopped into
   ½-inch pieces
1 cup chopped yellow onion
1 tablespoon minced garlic
½ cup ketchup
¼ cup dark molasses
¼ cup prepared mustard

⅓ cup bourbon
2 tablespoons brown sugar
2 tablespoons Worcestershire sauce
⅜ teaspoon hot sauce
2 (28-ounce) cans baked beans
Salt and pepper to taste

Prepare smoking packets for the grill by soaking mesquite or hickory chips in water to cover for 30 minutes; drain. Wrap the chips loosely in 4×4-inch pieces of foil and pierce several holes in the top to allow the smoke to escape. Place the packets in the bottom of the grill before preheating. Cook the bacon in a large sauté pan over medium heat for 10 minutes or until crisp, stirring occasionally. Add the onion and garlic. Sauté for 5 minutes or until soft. Add the ketchup, molasses, mustard, bourbon, brown sugar, Worcestershire sauce and hot sauce and mix well. Bring to a boil and reduce the heat. Simmer for 5 minutes. Rinse the beans and drain. Place in a 2-quart heatproof baking dish. Add the sauce and mix well. Place on a rack over the prepared grill. Grill for 1½ hours over indirect medium heat. Season with salt and pepper to taste. *Yield: 15 servings.*

MACARONI AND CHEESE WITH WHITE WINE

1½ cups uncooked elbow macaroni
3 to 4 tablespoons finely chopped
    onion
3 tablespoons butter
3 to 4 tablespoons flour
½ teaspoon salt
¼ teaspoon pepper

1 cup milk
½ cup dry white wine
¾ to 1 cup (3 to 4 ounces) shredded
    sharp Cheddar cheese
¾ to 1 cup (3 to 4 ounces) shredded
    Monterey Jack cheese
¼ cup bread crumbs

Cook the macaroni using the package directions. Rinse under cold running water; drain.

Sauté the onion in the butter in a 2-quart saucepan over low heat until soft. Add the flour, salt and pepper, stirring constantly. Stir in the milk and wine gradually. Cook over medium-low heat until thickened, stirring constantly. Add the Cheddar cheese and Monterey Jack cheese. Cook until the cheese melts, stirring constantly. Add the macaroni and mix well. Spoon into a buttered 2-quart baking dish. Cover the top with the bread crumbs. Bake at 350 degrees for 30 to 35 minutes. *Yield: 6 servings.*

MOLASSES BARS

½ teaspoon baking soda
1½ cups molasses
2 eggs
1½ cups sugar
¾ cup (1½ sticks) margarine,
    softened

4 cups flour
1 teaspoon salt
1 teaspoon ginger

Mix the baking soda and molasses in a small bowl. Beat the eggs, sugar and margarine in a mixing bowl. Stir in the molasses mixture. Add the flour, salt and ginger and stir to blend well. Spread evenly in 2 greased 12×18-inch baking pans. Bake at 350 degrees for 15 to 20 minutes or until the dough rises and then falls. Cool before cutting. *Yield: 48 servings.*

SORGHUM MAKING

Mule-drawn cane presses, steaming vats, and jugs filled with sorghum can be found each fall harvest season throughout Kentucky. You can witness sorghum processing at farms in Mennonite communities such as those in Allen County or at festivals in Hancock County, Morgan County, Daniel Boone National Forest, or the Appalachian Harvest Festival. The Mountain Home Place, nestled in the mountains above Paintsville Lake in Johnson County, is a living history farm of the 1850s, and sorghum making is included in the demonstrations of authentic farming and home life practices.

ORANGE HONEY YEAST ROLLS

2 envelopes dry yeast
1 cup orange juice, warmed
$^1/_4$ cup ($^1/_2$ stick) butter or margarine
$^1/_4$ cup honey
$^1/_4$ cup packed brown sugar
$1^1/_2$ teaspoons salt
2 eggs

$^1/_2$ cup cold water
1 cup quick-cooking or rolled oats
2 teaspoons grated orange zest
$4^1/_4$ to $4^3/_4$ cups sifted flour
2 tablespoons butter, melted
$^1/_2$ cup honey
Grated zest of 1 orange

Dissolve the yeast in the orange juice in a large bowl. Add $^1/_4$ cup butter, $^1/_4$ cup honey, brown sugar, salt and eggs and mix until smooth. Add the cold water. Beat for 2 minutes or until smooth. Add the oats, 2 teaspoons orange zest and enough flour to form a soft dough. Knead on a lightly floured surface for 10 minutes or until satiny smooth. Shape into a ball. Place in a greased bowl, turning to coat the surface. Let rise, covered, for 1 hour or until doubled in bulk. Punch the dough down. Shape into 24 rolls. Place in greased medium muffin cups. Brush with 2 tablespoons melted butter. Cover and let rise in a warm place for 45 minutes or until nearly doubled in bulk. Bake at 375 degrees for 12 to 15 minutes or until golden brown.

   Mix $^1/_2$ cup honey and grated zest of 1 orange in a small bowl. Brush over the warm rolls. *Yield: 24 servings.*

Mix honey with chopped nuts, cream cheese, or mashed bananas for cake filling or frosting. If using creamed honey, mix with dried fruit or chopped nuts.

EASY WHEAT ROLLS

4 to 6 cups whole wheat flour
$^1/_2$ cup unbleached flour
$^2/_3$ cup sugar
$^1/_2$ cup canola oil
2 teaspoons baking powder
$^1/_2$ teaspoon salt
$^1/_2$ teaspoon baking soda
$^1/_2$ cup honey or sorghum
$1^1/_2$ cups buttermilk

Combine 4 cups whole wheat flour, unbleached flour, sugar, canola oil, baking powder, salt, baking soda and honey in a large bowl and mix well. Stir in the buttermilk. Sprinkle the countertop with the remaining whole wheat flour. Knead the dough on the prepared counter until the dough is no longer sticky.

Divide the dough into 4 equal portions. Roll each portion into a circle $^1/_2$ inch thick. Cut into circles with a biscuit cutter. Place in ungreased baking pans. Bake at 375 degrees for 10 minutes or until light brown. (You may substitute a mixture of $1^1/_2$ cups milk and 2 to 3 tablespoons vinegar for the buttermilk.) *Yield: 30 servings.*

Honey should not be fed to infants less than two years of age. For older children and adults, honey is a safe and nutritious food.

193

APPALACHIAN GINGERBREAD

1 egg
1/2 cup sugar
1/2 cup (1 stick) butter, melted
1/2 teaspoon cinnamon
1/2 teaspoon cloves
1 teaspoon ginger

1 cup sorghum
1 cup hot water
2 cups flour
1 1/2 teaspoons baking soda
Sauce (below)

Beat the egg and sugar in a mixing bowl. Add the butter, cinnamon, cloves, ginger, sorghum and hot water and mix well. Stir in the flour and baking soda. Pour into a greased 9×13-inch baking pan. Bake at 350 degrees for 30 minutes.

To serve, cut into pieces and spoon the hot Sauce over the top.
Yield: 15 servings.

SAUCE

1 cup sugar
2 tablespoons cornstarch
1/8 teaspoon salt
1/8 teaspoon nutmeg

2 cups boiling water
1/4 cup (1/2 stick) margarine or butter
1/2 teaspoon vanilla extract

Mix the sugar, cornstarch, salt and nutmeg in a bowl. Add the boiling water and stir until the dry ingredients are dissolved. Add the margarine and vanilla and mix well until smooth. (For Lemon Sauce, add 1 1/2 tablespoons lemon juice.)
Yield: 15 servings.

Cynthiana Pecan Cake

1½ pounds pecan halves
1 (15-ounce) package raisins
2 cups finely cut candied orange peel
3 cups sifted flour
2 teaspoons baking powder
½ teaspoon salt

4 teaspoons nutmeg
1 cup (2 sticks) butter, softened
2¼ cups sugar
6 egg yolks
1 cup bourbon
6 egg whites, stiffly beaten

Cut each of the pecan halves into 3 crosswise slices. Rinse the raisins in hot water. Drain and pat dry on a towel. Mix the pecans, raisins and orange peel with 1 cup of the flour. Sift the remaining flour with the baking powder, salt and nutmeg.

Cream the butter and sugar in a very large mixing bowl. Beat the egg yolks in a mixing bowl until thick and pale yellow. Add to the creamed mixture and beat well. Add the sifted flour mixture alternately with the bourbon, beating until smooth after each addition. Fold in the pecan mixture gradually. Fold in the stiffly beaten egg whites. Spoon into a greased 10 inch angel food tube pan lined with brown paper and greased on both sides. Let stand for 10 minutes.

Steam, covered, in a large pan over medium-high heat for 2 hours. Bake at 300 degrees for 1 hour or until a cake tester inserted in the center comes out clean. Remove to a wire rack to cool partially. Remove the cake from the pan and turn right side up, leaving the brown paper on the cake. Let stand until cool. Wrap the cake tightly with foil. Chill in the refrigerator for a few days before serving. Store the cake in the refrigerator. (This cake is excellent to replace the traditional fruitcake.) *Yield: 30 servings.*

Bluegrass Bourbon

Nearly all of the nation's bourbon whiskey is produced here in Kentucky. Quality grain, clear limestone water, and white oak trees for barrels have provided the basic necessities for superior distilled spirits since the late 1700s. The "liquid" form of grain was then placed in a barrel and shipped down the Ohio and Mississippi Rivers to the world.

Today the Commonwealth has only nine operating distilleries located in Anderson, Franklin, Jefferson, Nelson, and Woodford counties, and many offer tours (call in advance).

WINE CAKE

1 (2-layer) package yellow cake mix
1 (3-ounce) package vanilla instant
    pudding mix
3/4 cup vegetable oil

3/4 cup sherry
1 teaspoon nutmeg
4 eggs

Combine the cake mix, pudding mix, oil, sherry, nutmeg and eggs in a mixing bowl and beat for 5 to 8 minutes at medium speed. Pour into a bundt pan sprayed with nonstick cooking spray. Bake at 350 degrees on the center oven rack for 50 minutes or until the cake tests done. Remove from the oven and cool in the pan for 10 minutes. Invert onto a wire rack to cool completely. (You may sprinkle with confectioners' sugar or use your favorite glaze.) *Yield: 15 servings.*

BOURBON BALLS

3 cups vanilla wafer crumbs
1 cup finely chopped pecans
1 cup confectioners' sugar

3 tablespoons light corn syrup
1/2 cup Kentucky bourbon
1/2 cup confectioners' sugar

Mix the vanilla wafer crumbs, pecans and 1 cup confectioners' sugar in a medium mixing bowl. Add the corn syrup and bourbon and stir to mix well. Shape into small balls. Roll in 1/2 cup confectioners' sugar to coat. Store in a foil-lined container in the refrigerator until ready to serve. (These are best if made several days ahead.) *Yield: 60 servings.*

Kentucky Hospitality Bourbon Balls

¹/₄ cup bourbon
2 cups finely chopped pecans
1 cup (2 sticks) butter, softened
1 (5-ounce) can evaporated milk
3 pounds confectioners' sugar
4 cups (24 ounces) semisweet chocolate chips

Pour the bourbon over the pecans in a bowl and toss to coat. Combine the butter, evaporated milk and confectioners' sugar in a bowl and blend well. Add the pecan mixture and knead well. Roll into 1-inch balls. Place on a tray. Chill until firm.

Temper the chocolate as directed at right. Dip the balls into the chocolate using a dipping fork or wooden pick and shake off the excess chocolate. Place on a tray lined with waxed paper. Let stand until cool. Place in individual petit-four packages. (You may substitute 4 cups of candy coating for the semisweet chocolate chips.) *Yield: 96 servings.*

Over 100 dozen candies were made with this recipe to present to attendees of the 1987 National Association of Extension Home Economists conference in Louisville, Kentucky.

Tempering Chocolate

To make chocolate suitable for dipping without the use of paraffin, it should be tempered so it will stay glossy and firm at room temperature. Begin by melting ²/₃ of your chocolate to 118 degrees so it melts but does not separate. Transfer the chocolate to a second bowl. Gradually add the remaining chocolate, some of it in large lumps, to the melted chocolate. By adding this new "tempered chocolate," it will cool and form the desired crystals needed for decorating and coating. Continue stirring in the pieces until it reaches a temperature of 88 degrees. Remove any remaining chocolate lumps and re-use to temper another batch of chocolate. At this point, the chocolate is ready to use. Do not allow the chocolate to cool to 77 degrees or the tempering process will need to be repeated.

Bourbon Brownies

3/4 cup flour
1 teaspoon baking soda
1/4 teaspoon salt
1/2 cup sugar
1/3 cup margarine
2 tablespoons water
1 cup (6 ounces) chocolate chips

1 teaspoon vanilla extract
2 eggs
1 1/2 cups pecan pieces
1/4 cup bourbon
White Bourbon Frosting (below)
1 cup (6 ounces) chocolate chips,
    melted

Sift the flour, baking soda and salt into a mixing bowl. Combine the sugar, margarine and water in a saucepan. Bring to a boil over low heat, stirring constantly. Remove from the heat. Add 1 cup chocolate chips and vanilla and stir until smooth. Add the eggs and beat well. Add to the flour mixture and mix well. Stir in the pecans. Spoon into a greased 9-inch baking pan. Bake at 325 degrees for 30 to 35 minutes or until the edges pull from the side of the pan. Remove from the oven and pierce holes in the brownies using wooden picks. Pour the bourbon over the top. Let stand until cool. Spread White Bourbon Frosting over the brownies. Spread the melted chocolate chips over the top to glaze. *Yield: 12 servings.*

White Bourbon Frosting

1/4 cup (1/2 stick) margarine, softened
2 cups confectioners' sugar
2 tablespoons bourbon
1 tablespoon water

Beat the margarine, confectioners' sugar, bourbon and water in a mixing bowl until smooth. *Yield: 12 servings.*

Sorghum Caramel Brownies

$1/2$ cup (1 stick) margarine, softened
$3/4$ cup packed brown sugar
2 eggs, beaten
$1/4$ cup sorghum
1 cup flour

$1/2$ teaspoon baking soda
$1/4$ teaspoon salt
1 cup chopped pecans
1 teaspoon vanilla extract

Cream the margarine and brown sugar in a mixing bowl until light and fluffy. Add the eggs and sorghum and mix well. Add the flour, baking soda and salt and beat until smooth. Stir in the pecans and vanilla. Pour into a greased 9×13-inch baking pan. Bake at 350 degrees for 20 to 25 minutes or until the edges pull from the side of the pan. *Yield: 15 servings.*

Energy Bars

2 cups rolled oats
1 cup raisins
3 cups crisp rice cereal
1 cup dry-roasted unsalted peanuts
1 cup roasted sunflower seeds

5 tablespoons margarine
$1/4$ cup honey
$1/2$ cup reduced-fat peanut butter
4 cups ($10^1/2$ ounces) miniature
    marshmallows

Spread the oats in a baking pan. Bake at 350 degrees for 8 to 9 minutes or until toasted. Combine the toasted oats, raisins, cereal, peanuts and sunflower seeds in a bowl and mix well.

    Melt the margarine, honey, peanut butter and marshmallows in a large saucepan over low heat, stirring constantly. Add the oat mixture and mix well. Press into a greased 9×13-inch pan. Chill, covered, in the refrigerator. (Use fresh marshmallows for best results. Do not use diet or reduced-fat margarine.) *Yield: 32 servings.*

County Court Days

When the traveling circuit judge came to the county seat each month to hear court cases, people would travel narrow, winding roads to gather for "court days." This became the day people traded mules, dogs, knives, equipment, and food items like fresh sorghum, fried fruit pies, and cream pull candy. Each October, Montgomery County holds a weekend-long "Court Day" festival reenacting this important event from Kentucky's past. Check out court days and festivals across the state for a great selection of local antiques, crafts, and delicious food.

Sorghum Crinkles

2 cups flour
$^1/_2$ teaspoon salt
2 teaspoons baking soda
1 teaspoon cinnamon
1 teaspoon ginger

$^2/_3$ cup vegetable oil
1 cup sugar
1 egg
$^1/_4$ cup sorghum or molasses
$^1/_4$ cup sugar

Mix the flour, salt, baking soda, cinnamon and ginger together. Combine the oil and 1 cup sugar in a large mixing bowl. Add the egg and beat well. Stir in the sorghum. Add the flour mixture and mix well. Shape the dough into 1-inch balls. Roll each ball in $^1/_4$ cup sugar. Place 2 inches apart on greased cookie sheets. Bake at 350 degrees for 10 to 12 minutes or until light brown. Remove to wire racks to cool. *Yield: 48 servings.*

Soft Sorghum Cookies

1 teaspoon ginger
1 teaspoon cinnamon
1 teaspoon sugar
1 tablespoon baking soda
$^1/_8$ teaspoon salt
5 cups flour

1 cup packed brown sugar
1 cup sorghum
1 cup shortening, melted
$^1/_2$ cup hot water
1 egg, lightly beaten

Mix the ginger, cinnamon, sugar, baking soda, salt and $^1/_2$ cup of the flour in a bowl. Add the remaining flour and mix well. Mix the brown sugar and sorghum in a large mixing bowl. Stir in the shortening and hot water. Add the egg and mix well. Add the flour mixture and mix to form a soft dough. Roll the dough $^1/_4$ inch thick on a floured surface. Cut into desired shapes with cookie cutters. Place on ungreased cookie sheets. Bake at 350 degrees for 10 to 12 minutes or until light brown. Remove to wire racks to cool. You may frost if desired. *Yield: 36 servings.*

Sorghum and Ginger Cookies

1 cup sorghum
1/2 cup water
1/2 cup (1 stick) butter or margarine
1/4 cup sugar
1 teaspoon baking soda

1/2 teaspoon salt
1 1/2 teaspoons ginger
3 cups sifted flour
Sugar for sprinkling (optional)

Heat the sorghum and water in a large saucepan to almost the boiling point. Remove from the heat. Add the butter and stir until the butter melts. Stir in a mixture of 1/4 cup sugar, baking soda, salt and ginger. Stir in enough flour to form a soft dough. Chill, covered, for 3 to 12 hours. Roll the dough 1/4 inch thick on a lightly floured surface. (Do not roll any thinner or the cookies will be hard and crisp.) Cut into desired shapes with a floured cookie cutter. Place on ungreased cookie sheets. Sprinkle with additional sugar. (For a heavy crust of sugar, brush lightly with a mixture of 1 egg and 1 tablespoon water and then sprinkle with sugar.) Bake at 350 degrees for 8 to 10 minutes or until brown. Watch closely to prevent burning. Remove to wire racks to cool. Store in an airtight container. *Yield: 15 servings.*

Kentucky Bourbon Dessert Sauce

1/2 cup (1 stick) butter
1 cup sugar

1 egg
1/3 cup bourbon

Melt the butter in a heavy saucepan over medium heat. Add the sugar. Cook for 3 minutes. Beat the egg in a mixing bowl. Add the butter mixture gradually, whisking constantly. Return to the saucepan. Cook for 2 minutes, whisking constantly. Remove from the heat. Whisk in the bourbon. Serve warm over bread pudding or ice cream. *Yield: 8 servings.*

Honey Sauce

2 tablespoons butter or margarine
1/4 cup honey
2 cups water
1/2 teaspoon salt
2 tablespoons cornstarch
1/2 cup raisins or seedless dates, chopped

Combine the butter, honey, water and salt in a saucepan and mix well. Mix 1/4 cup of the honey mixture with the cornstarch in a bowl. Add to the remaining honey mixture in the saucepan. Cook over medium heat until the mixture thickens and comes to a boil, stirring constantly. Boil for 2 to 3 minutes, stirring constantly. Remove from the heat. Stir in the raisins. Let stand until cool. (This is a nice sauce to serve over baked apples, puddings, pound cake, etc.)
Yield: 12 servings.

Girls' Canning Clubs were one of the predecessors of Kentucky 4-H in the early part of the twentieth century. With the rural population of the state and the dependency of farm families to produce their own food supply, safe food preservation techniques were important for all ages. County Extension Agents provided hands-on training for youth, as well as opportunities for exhibiting their work at county fairs.

RECIPE CONTRIBUTORS

Kimberly Adams
Lorie Adams
Gwenda Adkins
Rosie Allen
Grace M. Angotti
Carol Bailey
Jane Bailey
Jean Baugh
Jennifer Benham
Margaret S. Berg
Stephania Blair
Sara Bogle
Kelli Bonifer
Myra Braden
Ann Bradley
Sarah Ball Brandl
Kathy Brannon
Linda Brown
Belinda Bryant
Kathy Bryson
Nellie Buchanan
Elizabeth Buckner
Judy Burns
Georgia Burton
Cheryl Case
Chef Joe Castro
Janette Chapman
Ruth Chowning
Elaine Clift
Jean W. Cloar
Donna Clore
Brenda Cockerham
Jerri Cockrel
Debbie Colvin
Linda Combs
Brenda Cook
Debra Cotterill
Cretia Crowe
Isobel Crutchfield
Marian Davis
Chef Charles M. Dedman

Stephanie Derifield
Diana Doggett
Pam Dooley
Jan Dougan
Nancy Eckler
Nancy Edwards
Sheila Fawbush
Lucy Forbes
Chef John Foster
Judith Foster
Donna Fryman
Maryellen Garrison
Chef Jim Gerhardt
Carolyn Goodman
Kay Hall
Carolyn Ham
Jill Harris
Laura E. Heddleson
Peggy Helton
Myrna Herron
Judith Hetterman
Mary Hixson
Kaye Holbrook
Valerie Holland
Jennifer Howard
Lora Lee Frazier Howard
Theresa A. Howard
Theresa G. Howard
Nancy Hunt
Hazel Jackson
Brooke Jenkins
Janet Johnson
Nancy Jones
Connie Jones-Woolery
Kathy Jump
Nancy Kelley
Kay Kennedy
Alice P. Killpatrick
Liz Kingsland
Annie Kingston
Jennifer Klee

Kenna Knight
Chef Anthony Lamas
Virginia Langford
Martha Lee
Sally Lewis
Edith Lovett
Natasha Lucas
Loretta Lynn
Guynd Lyons
Chef Rex Lyons
Patricia Margolis
Joan Martin
Diane Mason
Rita May
Melanie Mays
Mindy McCulley
Chef Ouita Michel
Connie Minch
Sally Mineer
Louise Moore
Nelda Moore
Becky Nash
Judi O'Bryan
Tracy Overbey
Betty Overly
Marsha Parker
Debra Parrish
Martha Perkins
Tina Peter
Mildred Potts
Peggy Powell
Jane Proctor
Sandy Proffitt
Christy Ramey
Denise Rennekamp
Ronda Rex
Lillian Rice
Carole Rison
Chris Rivera
Mary Roenker
Kathy Roesel

Carolyn Royalty
Mary S. Saunooke
Margaret Scott
Theresa Scott
Debbie Shepherd
Pam Sigler
Phyllis Simmons
Evelyn Sinclair
M. Martha Slemp
Katie Smallwood
Rita Smart
Lida Smith
Michelle Smith
Chef Taylor Snedegar
Rita Spence
Martha Lee Stamper
Jane Steely
Linda P. Stephens
Laura Stephenson
Rita Stewart
Rowena Sullivan
Dr. Bonnie Tanner
Deborah Thompson
Sharon Thompson
Emma Tucker
Carol Vinyard
Chef Angie Vives
Chef Graham Waller
Geraldine Watson
Terry Whalen
Susan K. White-Sayers
Laura Wilson
Glenna Sue Wooten
Leslie Workman
Vicki Wynn
Pam York
Linda Young
Martha Yount
Suellen Zornes

PRIDE OF KENTUCKY RESOURCE GUIDE

Kentucky Department of Agriculture—www.kyagr.com

Capitol Annex, Suite 188 / Frankfort, KY 40601 / Phone: 502-564-5126 or
KDA Division of Market Research
100 Fair Oaks Lane, Suite 252 / Frankfort, KY 40601 / Phone: 502-564-4983

- *KDA Country Store web site allows you to shop for Kentucky food and products*
- *KDA Farm Store web site provides information on where to buy Kentucky livestock, hay, wood products, equipment, and services*
- *Farmers' Market Directory lists markets by county*
- *Kentucky Food Products Directory lists food products manufactured in Kentucky by product*
- *Kentucky Fresh and Buy Kentucky promotional campaign information*
- *Agri-Links web page with connections to the following: Agricultural Organizations, Ag Colleges and Universities, Marketing Resources, News and Publications, State and Federal Resources, and Equine Organizations*

Kentucky Farm Bureau Federation—www.kyfb.com

9201 Bunsen Parkway / P.O. Box 20700 / Louisville, KY 40250-0700
Phone: 502-495-5106

- *Certified Roadside Farm Market Program*
- *Brochure or web listing with map showing locations of farm markets and featured products throughout the state*
- *Listing of Roadside Farm Market Attractions*
- *Calendar of Roadside Farm Market Festivals*

Kentucky Tourism Commission—www.kentuckytourism.com

Kentucky Department of Travel
500 Mero Street, Suite 2200 / Frankfort, KY 40601 / Phone: 502-564-4930
- *Listing of festivals and special events*
- *Listing of tourism locations by county*

West Kentucky Corporation—www.thinkwestkentucky.com

P.O. Box 51153, Carroll Knicely Institute, WKU South Campus
Bowling Green, KY 42102 / Phone: 270-781-6858 or
P.O. Box 1428, MSU Collins Technology Center, Room 208
Murray, KY 42071 / Phone: 270-762-3294

- *Agritourism listing*
- *Barn Tours of Kentucky*
- *Agriculture Photo Contest*
- *Agriculture Newsletters*
- *Updates on legislative issues*
- *Links to Agribusiness and Commercial Associations*

The Governor's Office of Agricultural Policy (GOAP)—www.kyagpolicy.com

404 Ann Street / Frankfort, KY 40601 / Phone: 502-564-4627

- *Provides a direct link between the Governor and the state's agricultural industry*
- *Administers the Governor's Commission on Family Farms, the Kentucky Agricultural Resource Development Authority, the Governor's Tobacco Marketing and Export Advisory Council, the Kentucky Agricultural Development Board (Phase I), the Kentucky Tobacco Settlement Trust Corporation (Phase II), and the Kentucky Aquaculture Infrastructure Development Fund*
- *Represents Kentucky's interests as national agricultural policy is developed*

Additional Kentucky Food and Agriculture Resources

Kentucky Agriculture Directory

Available from Kentucky Department of Agriculture
Division of PR & Communications
500 Mero Street, 7th Floor / Frankfort, KY 40601
Booklet contains the following listings:

- *Agribusiness and Commercial Associations*
- *Agriculture Media, broadcast and print*
- *Agriculture Colleges and State Universities*
- *Area Development Districts*
- *Beef Associations*
- *County Extension Offices*
- *Dairy Associations*
- *Equine Organizations*
- *Farm Co-ops*
- *Farm Organizations*
- *Federal Government Agencies*
- *Kentucky U.S. Congressional Delegation*
- *State Government Agencies*
- *Tobacco Organizations*
- *Youth Organizations*

University of Kentucky Cooperative Extension Service—www.ca.uky.edu

- *Extension listing contains links to each County Extension Office in the state*
- *Agricultural and Natural Resources listing has information on Kentucky agriculture and links to partner groups and organizations*

Kentucky State University Cooperative Extension Program—www.kysu.edu/landgrant

400 E. Main Street / Frankfort, KY 40601 / Phone: 502-597-6310

- *Research and demonstration farm features Aquaculture, Apiculture, Horticulture, and Entomology projects*
- *Small Farmer Outreach Training and Technical Assistance programs*
- *"Third Thursday" Sustainable Agriculture Workshops*

Nutritional Guidelines and Profiles

The editors have attempted to present these family recipes in a format that allows approximate nutritional values to be computed. Persons with dietary or health problems or whose diets require close monitoring should not rely solely on the nutritional information provided. They should consult their physician or a registered dietitian for specific information.

Nutritional information for these recipes is computed from information derived from many sources, including materials supplied by the United States Department of Agriculture, computer databanks, and journals in which the information is assumed to be in the public domain. However, many specialty items, new products, and processed foods may not be available from these sources or may vary from the average values used in these profiles. More information on new and/or specific products may be obtained by reading the nutrient labels. Unless otherwise specified, the nutritional profile of these recipes is based on all measurements being level.

- Artificial sweeteners vary in use and strength and should be used to taste, using the recipe ingredients as a guideline. Sweeteners using aspartame (NutraSweet® and Equal®) should not be used as a sweetener in recipes involving prolonged heating, which reduces the sweet taste. For further information on the use of these sweeteners, refer to the package.
- Alcoholic ingredients have been analyzed for the basic information. Cooking causes the evaporation of alcohol, which decreases alcoholic and caloric content.
- Buttermilk, sour cream, and yogurt are the types available commercially.
- Canned beans and vegetables have been analyzed with the canning liquid. Rinsing and draining canned products will lower the sodium content.
- Chicken, cooked for boning and chopping, has been roasted; this method yields the lowest caloric values.
- Cottage cheese is cream-style with 4.2% creaming mixture. Dry curd cottage cheese has no creaming mixture.
- Eggs are all large. To avoid raw eggs that may carry salmonella, as in eggnog or 6-week muffin batter, use an equivalent amount of pasteurized egg substitute.
- Fat content of ground beef is 16%; 10% for extra-lean ground beef.
- Flour is unsifted all-purpose flour.
- Garnishes, serving suggestions, and other optional information are not included in the profile.
- Margarine and butter are regular, not whipped or presoftened.
- Milk is whole milk, 3.5% butterfat. Low-fat milk is 1% butterfat. Evaporated milk is whole milk with 60% of the water removed.
- Oil is any type of vegetable cooking oil. Shortening is hydrogenated vegetable shortening.
- Ingredients to taste have not been included in the nutritional profile.
- If a choice of ingredients has been given, the profile reflects the first option. If a choice of amounts has been given, the profile reflects the greater amount.

Nutritional Profiles

Pg. #	Recipe Title (Approx Per Serving)	Cal	Prot (g)	Carbo (g)	T Fat (g)	% Cal from Fat	Chol (mg)	Fiber (g)	Sod (mg)
11	Two-Way Shredded Beef[1]	310	37	2	16	48	127	<1	376
11	Tex-Mex Beef Wraps	915	82	56	37	36	254	4	1970
12	Honey Mustard Barbecue Beefwiches	547	41	49	18	31	127	1	1233
12	Company Pot Roast[1]	283	30	13	12	38	70	<1	1868
13	Fiesta Beef Pot Roast	362	13	55	8	21	49	2	962
13	Bellefont Beef Curry	346	31	13	19	49	72	2	1241
14	Easy Beef Tips	301	11	37	11	34	17	3	243
14	French Dip	516	42	55	13	24	80	3	2133
15	Roast Beef Cheddar Pockets[1]	506	18	39	29	54	67	1	1037
15	Slow Cooker Stew	187	13	21	5	25	37	3	313
16	Blue Ribbon Tenderloin Steaks with Red Pepper Jelly	204	23	8	8	37	67	<1	132
16	Bourbon Steak[2]	407	40	17	16	36	96	<1	1496
17	Marinated Grilled Flank Steak[2]	264	24	5	15	52	54	<1	798
17	Stuffed Rolled Steak	382	41	29	10	24	97	2	1545
18	Round Steak Sauerbraten	140	19	4	4	29	48	<1	362
18	Pleasant Home Swiss Steak	227	27	10	9	35	64	1	491
19	Smothered Swiss Steak	270	27	17	11	35	64	1	411
19	Madras Beef Curry	148	16	8	6	38	42	1	1001
20	Sonaran Beef Steak	793	23	24	67	76	100	1	778
20	Ground Beef and Asparagus Pasta Toss	482	29	28	28	52	78	3	153
21	Kentucky Cottage Beef Bake	364	22	25	19	48	90	1	755
22	Beef Spaghetti Casserole	305	22	14	18	53	67	1	228
22	Silver Grove Sensational Stroganoff	469	26	16	34	65	100	2	1446
23	Microwave Lasagna	267	19	17	14	47	63	2	1016
23	Metcalfe Meatballs	340	17	45	11	29	66	2	884
24	Meat Loaf with Sauce	256	19	16	13	45	83	1	807
25	Family Favorite Meat Loaf	184	13	10	10	48	75	<1	364
25	Eden Shale Sloppy Joes	301	17	29	14	40	46	4	584
26	Claysville Cabbage Rolls	253	16	12	15	55	50	2	803
29	Cinnamon Apple Pork Roast	310	30	21	12	35	84	1	72
29	Pork Loin Roast with Bourbon Glaze	532	55	31	18	31	158	1	132
30	Kentucky Garlic and Rosemary Pork Tenderloin[1]	292	34	2	15	49	102	<1	97
30	Holiday Pork Tenderloin	437	45	32	13	28	126	1	296
31	Grilled Pork Tenderloin[2]	362	32	5	24	59	84	<1	1285

NUTRITIONAL PROFILES

Pg. #	Recipe Title (Approx Per Serving)	Cal	Prot (g)	Carbo (g)	T Fat (g)	% Cal from Fat	Chol (mg)	Fiber (g)	Sod (mg)
31	Barbecued Pork on Buns	395	24	39	16	36	70	2	1041
32	Pork Fajitas[2]	425	30	47	13	27	63	4	672
32	Pork Fried Rice	329	16	36	13	35	137	1	719
33	Baked Stuffed Pork Chops[1]	285	30	16	10	34	79	1	520
33	Pork Chop Bake	470	30	64	11	20	62	6	855
34	West Kentucky-Style Barbecued Pork Chops[1]	212	21	6	11	49	61	1	1324
34	Orange Pork Chops	546	50	37	20	34	129	1	599
35	Pork Chop Potato Casserole	453	28	32	23	47	75	3	703
35	Pork Chops with Wild Rice	352	29	31	12	31	63	3	1301
36	Sausage Blueberry Breakfast Cake	407	8	49	21	45	23	2	436
37	Breakfast Soufflé	197	11	13	11	50	30	<1	457
37	Goetta[3]	191	8	26	7	31	11	4	464
38	Kentucky Sausage and Corn Casserole	384	11	44	19	43	35	4	831
38	Pork Sausage Ring	278	13	14	19	61	46	1	882
39	Country Ham	350	49	11	11	29	107	<1	2609
39	Kentucky Ham Slices	340	21	54	5	12	47	0	1150
40	Country Ham Cheesecake	215	5	13	16	66	37	<1	360
41	Country Ham Cups	156	7	13	8	49	18	1	373
41	Kentucky Hot Brown	692	41	23	48	63	224	1	1693
42	Slow-Cooked Fresh Ham with Dijon Chardonnay	452	53	7	19	38	109	1	4588
42	Ham and Cheese Bundles	174	9	11	9	51	22	0	276
43	Breakfast Ham Casserole	188	17	14	7	35	31	1	210
43	Ham and Sweet Potato Casserole	558	20	93	12	20	63	4	130
44	Chef Jim's Famous Pork Sandwich	489	53	31	16	30	105	3	2804
47	Kentucky Rosemary Lemon Baked Chicken[1]	617	72	8	32	48	220	3	244
48	Herb-Roasted Chicken and Potatoes	316	36	19	11	31	99	3	488
49	Chicken and Corn Bread Dressing[1]	245	19	20	9	35	47	2	130
50	Loretta's Famous Chicken and Dumplin's[1]	330	27	29	11	30	84	1	306
51	Cropper Chicken	533	28	69	17	28	79	2	872
51	Working Woman's Chicken Potpie	374	14	35	19	47	47	2	924
52	Marrowbone Barbecued Chicken Breasts	625	36	38	35	50	91	1	1038
53	Kentucky Barbecue Chicken[1]	181	27	3	6	31	81	<1	863
54	Buttermilk Pecan Chicken	455	33	17	29	57	101	3	1110
54	Microwave Pineapple Chicken[1]	270	15	52	2	6	37	2	711

NUTRITIONAL PROFILES

Pg. #	Recipe Title (Approx Per Serving)	Cal	Prot (g)	Carbo (g)	T Fat (g)	% Cal from Fat	Chol (mg)	Fiber (g)	Sod (mg)
55	Rolled Chicken Breasts[4]	436	33	36	17	36	159	1	215
56	Chicken Broccoli Casserole	451	40	11	27	54	123	2	898
56	Chicken Celery Casserole	463	26	29	27	53	96	1	704
57	Potluck Pleasing Chicken Casserole	411	19	14	31	68	127	1	1436
58	Almond Chicken Francais	427	25	34	20	43	80	4	427
59	Hooktown Herb Chicken Alfredo	338	28	10	20	54	88	1	661
59	Herbed Chicken Pasta	584	43	82	9	13	67	6	725
60	Chicken Tetrazzini	662	47	58	24	34	93	4	1912
60	Curried Chicken Pâté	49	3	1	4	69	14	<1	61
61	Fruited Chicken Salad	489	19	27	34	63	54	2	405
61	Lillian's Chicken Salad	252	11	13	18	62	32	1	194
62	Hot Chicken Salad	211	13	3	16	68	48	1	360
62	Hot Turkey Salad	362	17	21	23	57	143	3	648
63	Apple Cider Baked Turkey Breast	509	71	10	18	33	182	<1	819
63	Miniature Turkey Meat Loaves	268	28	8	13	45	103	<1	463
64	Turkey Shiitake Burgers	413	45	7	21	48	164	1	401
64	Compton's Mini Hot Browns	26	2	2	1	49	4	<1	63
65	Morgan Cheese and Egg Salad Spread	345	12	5	30	80	188	<1	820
65	Eggs for a Crowd	199	11	3	16	73	330	0	547
66	Pasta Vegetable Scramble	366	24	50	7	18	216	4	2996
67	Old-Time Lemon "Cheese Cake"	1095	13	134	58	47	381	2	800
68	White Chocolate Lemon Mousse Pie	618	5	47	48	68	284	<1	311
69	Egg Custard Pie	348	4	37	21	54	81	1	277
69	Sawdust Pie	676	9	77	39	51	41	5	308
70	Maysville's Historic Transparent Pie	555	5	63	32	52	178	1	276
70	No-Weep Meringue	34	1	7	0	0	0	<1	57
81	Shrimp Scampi	393	26	1	32	72	236	<1	1014
81	Montgomery County Lemon Shrimp	249	24	20	8	30	177	6	1120
82	Fresh Water Shrimp on Sweet Potato Bed[1]	432	7	62	19	39	72	3	334
83	Shrimp Casserole	307	20	33	10	31	144	2	1053
84	Nuevo Latino Shrimp and Grits	1450	64	161	67	40	309	5	2326
85	Smoked Cheddar Chipotle Sweet Corn Grit Cake[5]	1227	40	156	55	39	97	4	944
85	Oven-Roasted Onion and Tomato Salsa	65	1	4	6	74	0	1	573
86	Shrimp Pilau[1]	229	16	24	7	29	126	1	809

Nutritional Profiles

Pg. #	Recipe Title (Approx Per Serving)	Cal	Prot (g)	Carbo (g)	T Fat (g)	% Cal from Fat	Chol (mg)	Fiber (g)	Sod (mg)
86	Sautéed Shrimp	836	28	47	60	63	331	2	370
87	Shrimp Creole	161	12	13	8	41	88	3	1061
87	Grilled Black Bass with Sesame Seeds	208	17	1	15	66	54	<1	252
88	Tasty Catfish Dip	303	22	1	23	69	97	0	292
88	Blackened Catfish Fillets	423	27	1	34	73	153	<1	1571
89	Catfish in a Brown Bag	284	25	5	17	55	97	1	1062
89	Purchase Pan-Fried Catfish[1]	254	23	13	12	42	61	1	1131
90	Southern Fried Spoonfish	466	29	40	22	41	71	5	1634
91	Parmesan Catfish	451	45	13	24	48	151	1	1177
91	Trout Worcestershire	190	24	3	8	41	66	<1	338
91	LaRue Leg of Lamb	244	35	2	9	36	106	0	780
92	Grilled Lamb Chops[2]	139	15	10	5	29	44	<1	1356
92	Grilled Teriyaki Lamb Chops[2]	227	28	9	8	34	80	<1	949
93	Lamb Kabobs[2]	531	29	30	33	56	76	1	2481
93	Minted Lamb Loaf	272	22	8	17	56	117	1	376
94	Chevon Kabobs	167	26	3	5	29	71	<1	278
94	Baked Rabbit	623	87	9	24	36	244	2	534
95	Barbecued Rabbit[1]	384	30	26	18	42	85	1	1013
96	Slow Cooker Mount St. Joseph Burgoo	116	10	15	2	16	21	3	85
99	Spicy Two-Cheese Garden Appetizer	114	11	10	3	25	16	<1	515
99	Campbellsville Cheese Ball	111	4	1	11	83	25	<1	100
100	Glendale Goat Cheese with Strawberry Vinaigrette	971	21	47	80	73	91	4	600
101	Caraway Cheese Crisps	95	4	5	7	65	20	<1	121
101	Icy Tomato Buttermilk Soup	59	3	10	1	18	2	1	282
102	Autumn Cheesy Soup	449	24	16	32	65	100	1	1130
102	Taylor Cheesy Potato Soup	353	17	34	19	45	43	3	1868
103	Eggplant, Tomato and Goat Cheese Sandwiches	451	18	58	17	33	20	6	748
103	Buttermilk Salad	120	2	21	3	22	1	<1	60
104	Eighty-Eight Four-Cheese Eggplant Lasagna	264	17	37	8	24	22	6	1006
105	Blender Cheese Soufflé	293	14	11	22	67	164	<1	681
105	Cow Days Cottage Cheese Soufflé	140	9	17	4	27	92	<1	246
106	Cheese Casserole	188	8	10	13	61	106	<1	379
107	Cheese Ring	144	8	6	10	61	70	<1	212
107	Poplar Plains Cheese Pudding	248	16	10	16	58	148	<1	750

NUTRITIONAL PROFILES

Pg. #	Recipe Title (Approx Per Serving)	Cal	Prot (g)	Carbo (g)	T Fat (g)	% Cal from Fat	Chol (mg)	Fiber (g)	Sod (mg)
108	Gravel Switch Twist Cheese Bread	169	8	20	7	36	26	1	378
109	Cheddar Cheese Casserole Bread	221	8	33	6	25	18	1	173
109	Bagdad Breakfast Casserole	188	11	7	13	61	112	<1	430
110	Secret Family Recipe Banana Pudding	428	7	77	12	24	95	2	227
110	Southern Lassies	138	2	14	9	58	23	1	55
111	Pulled Cream Candy	61	<1	12	2	24	6	0	23
111	Old-Fashioned Brown Sugar Icing	266	1	41	12	39	23	<1	87
112	Vanilla Ice Cream	231	6	33	9	33	70	<1	149
112	Buttermilk Pie	410	5	52	21	45	112	1	325
113	Butterscotch Pie	442	6	73	15	30	88	1	228
114	Chess Pie	399	4	51	21	46	86	1	256
114	Bandana Peach Pie	480	6	45	32	59	82	2	218
117	Apple Broccoli Soy Salad	214	2	17	16	66	0	2	95
118	Hail Caesar Salad[2]	348	24	26	16	43	37	6	537
118	Green Soybeans and Corn	123	7	15	4	29	4	4	39
119	Vegi-Sausage Corn Bread	236	10	25	12	43	8	3	657
119	Benton Tofu Banana Bread	257	5	33	13	44	0	2	166
120	Fiesta Roll-Ups	477	28	60	15	27	25	6	966
120	Tofu Enchiladas	267	12	18	17	55	38	2	190
121	Soy Food Lasagna Delight	513	34	33	29	49	98	5	1289
122	Susan's Tofu Stir-Fry	498	30	78	8	15	0	10	535
123	Dreamy Strawberry Tofu	166	4	18	10	51	0	1	46
124	Cherry Tofu Delight	130	3	16	5	37	9	1	63
124	Chocolate Tofu Swirl Cheesecake	532	14	60	26	44	123	1	511
125	Pumpkin Tofu Pie	209	4	29	9	39	2	2	128
125	Broccoli Corn Bread	128	4	10	8	57	47	1	244
126	Cayce Corn Bread	291	6	21	21	65	65	2	421
126	Traditional Hot Water Corn Bread[3]	131	5	27	1	7	1	3	180
127	Old-Fashioned Stone-Ground Corn Bread	168	6	31	3	14	28	3	424
127	Light and Tasty Corn Cakes	67	2	7	4	48	20	1	64
128	Cumberland Cornmeal Muffins	123	3	17	5	33	19	2	234
128	Kentucky Spoon Bread	170	7	16	9	47	107	1	457
129	Old Time Turkey Corn Bread Dressing[1]	186	7	24	7	34	85	2	473
129	Boone Corn Bread Salad	364	12	35	20	48	18	6	949

NUTRITIONAL PROFILES

Pg. #	Recipe Title (Approx Per Serving)	Cal	Prot (g)	Carbo (g)	T Fat (g)	% Cal from Fat	Chol (mg)	Fiber (g)	Sod (mg)
130	Caramel Candy Corn	290	5	37	15	46	0	3	274
130	Microwave Caramel Corn	147	1	24	6	35	0	1	190
131	Shiloh Sweet Popcorn	192	<1	29	9	41	25	<1	101
131	Butler Beer Bread	135	3	27	<1	2	0	1	398
132	Horse Cave Dilly Bread	169	7	28	3	16	28	1	670
135	Mays Lick Cream of Asparagus Soup	264	11	15	19	62	50	3	864
136	Bluegrass Asparagus Quiche	406	17	22	28	61	166	1	528
136	Leather Britches	106	3	5	9	71	10	2	108
137	Sweet-and-Sour Green Beans	78	2	13	2	23	3	3	344
137	Harvard Beets	122	1	22	4	27	10	2	298
138	Big Creek Broccoli Salad[1]	416	6	39	28	58	4	4	538
138	Broccoli Raisin Salad[1]	297	5	40	15	43	14	3	292
139	Broccoli Platter	183	6	11	15	66	20	4	181
139	Scalloped Cabbage	99	3	9	6	52	16	1	587
140	Spiced Red Cabbage	80	1	15	3	27	0	3	396
140	Morehead Marinated Carrots[1]	329	3	60	11	28	0	5	314
141	Carrot Pineapple Cake with Walnut Cream Cheese Frosting	423	4	48	25	52	56	1	283
142	Beaumont Inn's Corn Pudding	232	9	21	13	48	138	1	446
142	Cadiz Cucumber Salad[1]	363	2	91	<1	1	<1	2	2361
143	Almond Bibb Salad[1]	185	3	17	13	61	0	2	213
144	Wolfe Wilted Lettuce[1]	213	4	6	18	82	23	2	386
144	Stuffed Mushrooms	191	5	17	12	54	15	1	381
145	Estill Shiitake Soup	46	2	8	<1	6	<1	2	883
145	Rigatoni with Shiitake Mushrooms and Kielbasa	325	8	34	18	50	9	2	148
146	Pickled Dilled Okra[1]	21	1	6	<1	3	0	2	1705
146	Bowling Green Pepper Casserole	424	18	21	30	63	65	2	708
147	Baked Potato Soup	583	16	32	44	67	58	2	1020
147	Party Potato Salad	250	4	35	11	39	77	2	470
148	Spicy Red Potato Salad	365	8	34	24	56	98	4	278
148	Roasted Potato Salad	232	5	34	11	40	0	4	112
149	Crusty Garlic Rosemary Potatoes	187	6	41	3	14	0	5	<1
150	Pulaski Pumpkin Corn Soup[1]	138	5	17	7	41	20	3	525
150	Pumpkin Bread	171	2	26	7	35	24	1	181
151	Toasted Pumpkin Seeds	105	4	3	9	74	0	1	3

NUTRITIONAL PROFILES

Pg. #	Recipe Title (Approx Per Serving)	Cal	Prot (g)	Carbo (g)	T Fat (g)	% Cal from Fat	Chol (mg)	Fiber (g)	Sod (mg)
151	Rhubarb Pie	437	3	66	18	37	72	1	312
152	Strawberry Spinach Salad[1]	238	4	19	18	64	0	3	48
152	Spinach Salad[1]	415	7	29	32	67	84	4	172
153	Butternut Squash Bread	259	4	43	9	31	36	2	273
153	Baked Summer Squash	216	5	20	14	55	84	4	542
154	Grandma's Cushaw Pie	301	7	39	13	39	70	1	341
154	Sweet Potatoes Stuffed with Apples	389	2	74	12	26	0	7	178
155	Sweet Potato Casserole	812	9	136	28	30	223	4	345
155	Sweet Potato Custard Pie	272	3	33	14	47	29	2	203
156	Taylor Made Salsa	29	1	6	<1	12	0	2	383
156	Tomato and Chipotle Salsa	62	1	10	3	37	0	2	53
157	Fresh Tomato and Basil Ring	173	8	7	13	66	29	1	152
157	Fayette Fried Green Tomatoes[1]	193	4	23	10	45	9	2	261
158	Tomato Pesto Tart	337	8	16	26	71	37	2	387
158	Basil Pesto	145	7	11	8	50	9	9	137
159	Tomato Jam	637	4	161	2	2	0	5	42
159	Oven-Fried Zucchini	60	2	7	3	41	1	1	321
160	Zucchini with Salsa	26	2	6	<1	8	0	2	7
160	Cobell Zucchini Combo	111	4	6	9	68	3	2	352
161	Zucchini Tomato Sauté over Spaghetti	196	6	27	8	34	5	4	338
161	Zucchini Relish[1]	225	2	57	<1	1	0	2	1458
162	Zucchini Bread	154	3	20	7	41	27	2	169
162	Chocolate Zucchini Cake	722	7	97	36	44	89	2	443
163	Vegetable Chowder	271	8	22	17	57	21	2	825
163	Vegetable Pie	307	5	21	23	67	16	2	324
164	Double Apple Salad	176	2	22	10	49	2	2	47
164	Mays Lick Apple Salad	309	4	31	20	56	28	2	119
165	Apple Cider Pancakes	169	4	33	2	11	7	2	400
165	Woodford Slow Cooker Apple Butter	105	<1	27	<1	3	0	2	<1
166	Woodford Mulled Cider	86	0	22	0	0	0	0	15
166	Beda Brown Betty	474	3	77	19	34	<1	3	477
167	Smith Grove Apple Macaroons	187	2	32	6	29	34	3	411
167	Apple Nut Pudding	295	5	43	13	37	71	3	522
168	Fresh Apple Cake with Brown Sugar Icing	380	3	41	24	55	27	2	179

NUTRITIONAL PROFILES

Pg. #	Recipe Title (Approx Per Serving)	Cal	Prot (g)	Carbo (g)	T Fat (g)	% Cal from Fat	Chol (mg)	Fiber (g)	Sod (mg)
169	Johnson County Apple Layer Cake with Coconut Pecan Frosting	620	6	89	28	40	56	2	372
170	Edna Smith's Old-Fashioned Stack Cake with Apple Filling	691	8	126	18	23	54	4	370
171	Edna Smith's Old-Fashioned Stack Cake with Strawberry Filling	652	8	115	18	25	54	3	350
172	Dried Apple Stack Cake	696	9	131	17	21	77	5	537
173	Old-Fashioned Pastry Apple Bars[1]	252	2	38	10	37	12	2	134
174	Ollie Pearl's Stacked Hand Apple Pies	361	1	43	20	51	20	1	379
175	Travellers Rest Apple Freezer Pie	458	3	68	20	39	41	2	222
175	Fresh Blackberry Cake	239	3	31	12	44	27	2	202
176	Washington Jam Cake with Brown Sugar Icing	724	6	115	28	34	93	1	259
177	Berry Almond Streusel	225	3	41	7	25	12	5	149
177	Blueberry Spice Jam	80	<1	21	<1	1	0	<1	3
178	High Bridge Blueberry Crisp	308	3	53	11	31	27	4	252
178	Blueberry Pound Cake	368	8	69	8	18	73	2	300
179	Blueberry Dessert	440	2	71	18	36	46	2	275
179	Grape Plum Jelly[1]	54	<1	14	<1	2	0	<1	1
180	Easy Peach Cobbler	393	3	70	12	27	34	2	250
180	Strawberry Rhubarb Jelly[1]	42	<1	11	<1	1	0	<1	<1
181	Sunrise Strawberry Pie	221	2	38	7	29	0	2	125
181	Strawberry Salsa	142	1	9	12	73	0	2	180
182	Wilder Watermelon Salsa	36	<1	9	<1	5	0	1	100
182	Farmers' Market Fruit	358	2	91	1	2	0	4	8
185	Kentucky Bourbon Nog	236	4	22	4	15	17	0	60
185	Bourbon Slush	142	<1	27	<1	0	0	<1	4
186	Kentucky Wine Cooler	118	<1	15	<1	0	0	<1	12
186	Hot Spiced Wine	72	<1	8	<1	1	0	<1	5
187	French Onion Soup	410	15	44	16	36	40	4	605
187	Lemon Chicken Breasts	274	27	1	13	44	73	<1	212
188	Bourbonnaise Barbecue Sauce	814	5	164	1	1	0	1	5869
188	Basic Barbecue Sauce	70	3	15	1	13	0	2	225
189	Honey Marinade for Steak	44	1	5	3	52	0	<1	702
189	Honey Orange Glaze for Ham	21	<1	5	<1	0	0	<1	<1
190	Honey French Dressing	124	<1	12	9	62	0	<1	98
190	Bourbon Barbecued Beans[1]	181	6	31	4	19	4	6	631
191	Macaroni and Cheese with White Wine	371	15	30	20	48	57	1	531

NUTRITIONAL PROFILES

Pg. #	Recipe Title (Approx Per Serving)	Cal	Prot (g)	Carbo (g)	T Fat (g)	% Cal from Fat	Chol (mg)	Fiber (g)	Sod (mg)
191	Molasses Bars	111	2	19	3	27	9	1	98
192	Orange Honey Yeast Rolls	175	4	32	4	19	25	1	182
193	Easy Wheat Rolls	161	4	29	4	23	<1	3	107
194	Appalachian Gingerbread	271	4	43	10	32	31	2	248
195	Cynthiana Pecan Cake	422	5	48	24	48	59	4	148
196	Wine Cake	300	3	34	16	49	57	<1	343
196	Bourbon Balls	52	<1	7	2	35	<1	<1	15
197	Kentucky Hospitality Bourbon Balls	125	1	19	6	39	5	1	22
198	Bourbon Brownies	406	4	45	24	50	35	2	269
199	Sorghum Caramel Brownies	201	3	21	13	55	28	1	165
199	Energy Bars	162	4	20	8	44	0	1	74
200	Sorghum Crinkles	71	1	10	3	40	4	<1	78
200	Soft Sorghum Cookies	156	3	23	6	34	6	1	118
201	Sorghum and Ginger Cookies	194	4	30	7	31	16	2	224
201	Kentucky Bourbon Dessert Sauce	228	1	25	12	46	57	0	124
202	Honey Sauce	61	<1	12	2	26	5	<1	117

[1]Nutritional information includes the entire amount of ingredients.
[2]Nutritional information includes the entire amount of marinade.
[3]Nutritional information does not include the vegetable oil for frying.
[4]Nutritional information does not include canola oil for deep-frying.
[5]Nutritional information does not include olive oil for frying.

INDEX

INDEX

INDEX

INDEX

INDEX

INDEX

Index

PRIDE OF KENTUCKY

GREAT RECIPES WITH FOOD, FARM, AND FAMILY TRADITIONS

Carol Rison
Bath County Cooperative Extension Service
53 Miller Drive
Owingsville, Kentucky 40360-2212
FAX: 1-606-674-6687

YOUR ORDER	QUANTITY	TOTAL
Pride of Kentucky $27.95 per book		$
Kentucky residents add $1.68 sales tax		$
Postage and handling at $5.00 per book		$
	TOTAL	$

VISA _____   MasterCard _____   Account Number _____

Signature _____   Exp. Date _____

Make checks payable to: *Pride of Kentucky*.

_____
Name

_____
Address

_____
City   State   Zip

_____
Telephone

Photocopies will be accepted.